OXFORD MEDICAL PUBLICATIONS

ADHD

the**facts**

ADHD
the**facts**

Mark Selikowitz

Consultant Developmental Pediatrician

Sydney, Australia

OXFORD
UNIVERSITY PRESS

OXFORD
UNIVERSITY PRESS

Great Clarendon Street, Oxford, OX2 6DP

Oxford University Press is a department of the University of Oxford.
It furthers the University's objective of excellence in research,
scholarship, and education by publishing worldwide in

Oxford   New York

Auckland   Bangkok   Buenos Aires   Cape Town   Chennai   Dar es Salaam   Delhi
Hong Kong   Istanbul   Karachi   Kolkata   Kuala Lumpur   Madrid   Melbourne   Mexico City
Mumbai   Nairobi   São Paulo   Shanghai Taipei   Tokyo   Toronto

Oxford is a registered trade mark of Oxford University Press
in the UK and in certain other countries

Published in the United States
by Oxford University Press Inc., New York

A catalogue record for this title is available from the British Library

ISBN 0 19 852628 8
1

Typeset by Cepha Imaging Pvt Ltd
Printed in Great Britain
on acid-free paper by Clays Ltd, Bungay, Suffolk

Preface

Awareness of attention-deficit/hyperactivity disorder (ADHD) has been growing among both parents and professionals over the past decade. Television programs and newspaper and magazine articles increasingly deal with this common and important condition.

Despite this media coverage, ignorance about ADHD is widespread. This book aims to help overcome such ignorance. It provides a practical overview of ADHD for all those who, in the broadest sense of the term, care for children. It will interest parents, teachers, doctors, and psychologists. It will also be of interest to the many other professionals, such as speech therapists and occupational therapists, who come into regular contact with children who struggle to learn, or have difficulty behaving appropriately for their age.

But if this book merely provides information, it will only partially have fulfilled its purpose. If children with ADHD and their parents are to be helped, knowledge alone will not suffice; it is essential that attitudes to children with this 'hidden handicap' change.

It is, therefore, my hope that this book will lead its readers to a reappraisal of the way we interpret the developmental difficulties that so many children in our community face. It is hoped that we will banish useless words, such as 'lazy', 'stupid', and 'naughty', in favor of alternatives that lead us to a deeper understanding of these children, of the difficulties they contend with, and of their special needs. We will also have to appreciate how stressful such children can be to live with, so that we can provide their parents with the support they need.

Section 1 and Sections 3 to 7 of the book cover ADHD in a general way. These sections will interest all parents.

In Section 2, each of the eight chapters is devoted to a specific area of development, and parents can select those chapters that are relevant to their child's particular difficulties.

To avoid using the cumbersome 'he or she' when referring to the child with ADHD, I have used 'he' in some sections and 'she' in others. All statements apply equally to both sexes unless otherwise specified.

I am grateful to the parents of David, Martine, Peter, and Greg who let me quote from their stories.

I am indebted to my friend and colleague, Dr Rory McCarthy, with whom I share the approach to the diagnosis and management of

ADHD that is reflected in this text. The book has benefited from the regular exchange of ideas that working with Rory makes possible.

Finally, I thank my wife, Jill, who proofread the first draft of the typescript and made many valuable comments and suggestions. Her perspective as a teacher and a parent has been of great value. This book is dedicated to her, and to my children, Daniel and Anne, with love.

November 2003   MS

the**facts**

CONTENTS

Section 5
Multi-modal treatment

Section 6

Section 7
Adulthood

Section 1

Introduction

1

What is ADHD?

A tale of two children

Dear Doctor

I am writing this letter to you before the appointment because I always find it difficult to remember what I wanted to say when I am sitting in front of a doctor.

We are desperate about David [age 7 years] – you are our last resort! We have been to numerous doctors, psychologists, and psychiatrists already. They all make us feel that we are the cause of David's problem. We are tired of being analysed – we just want help.

David has been difficult from the moment he was born. The first two of our children were easy babies; but David was irritable from the very beginning. He hardly slept as an infant. He walked earlier than our other two, and from the time he took his first steps at 9 months he has been on the go. As a toddler he was into everything and had to be watched all the time. We tried him on a 'hyperactivity diet', but it did not help. Now that he is older, he is not as active, but he still never seems to tire, except when he is sick. I feel guilty admitting that it is only when he is ill that I enjoy having him at home.

He is like a walking disaster. He takes risks all the time; he has broken his leg twice and has numerous scars. He acts without stopping to think of the consequences, and he never seems to learn from his mistakes.

He won't do as he is told and if we try to discipline him, he becomes abusive and even aggressive. We have tried 'timeout' [putting him in his room, when disobedient, to cool down], but he destroys his room so it is just not worth it. On two occasions he jumped out of his bedroom window and ran away.

Living with David is like walking on eggshells. The slightest frustration sets him off into a rage. But sometimes he will be aggressive for no apparent reason. For example, yesterday his brother was sitting watching television and David came into the room, walked up to him and kicked him – out of the blue! He seemed sorry after he had done it, but I can't understand why he does things like that.

Each morning I wake up and get out of bed with a feeling of trepidation waiting to see what kind of a mood he is in, and what sort of a day we can expect.

But even if he is in a good mood, it can change quite suddenly as the least thing sets him off.

Today is Saturday, and this morning he seemed all right, but then when he found his favourite T-shirt was in the wash, he started nagging and wanted to take it off the washing-line and wear it while it was still wet. I could not get him to see reason and he went on nagging for over an hour. Later, when I turned my back, he took it off the line and put it on. When I tried to take it off him, he started kicking and screaming and I just had to leave him alone. He is now in his room sobbing and kicking the door – we are in for another terrible weekend!

School has been a disaster for David. After the first week his teacher called me in to tell me he was impossible to teach. He wanders about the classroom; he calls out in class; he is noisy and he disrupts other children; his books are terribly messy; his work is never completed. The worst thing is that he is very rude to the teachers. He is easily affronted and takes any attempt to discipline him as a personal insult. He always seems to be getting punished, but it does not help. Earlier this term he was suspended from school for a week for swearing at a teacher. I had to take off work to stay with him, but I think he actually enjoyed the punishment.

He does not get on with the other children in the playground. He is very bossy with them and is not prepared to compromise. He has now earned a reputation as a bully, and is ostracised by the other children. He seems to get into punch-ups every day. I am sure he starts most of these. He will take on children who are older and larger than himself, so he often comes off second best. He was suspended from school for a week last term for punching a boy. The punishment made no difference to David – he was in a fight on his first day back!

I don't want you to think that David is always bad. He can be sweet and loving, and often he shows he is genuinely sorry for what he has done. But it never lasts for long – with David, trouble is always around the corner. Most worrying to us now is that David seems to be becoming depressed about his difficulties. Over the last month he has started saying that he is 'dumb'. He often says, 'Mummy, I don't know what is wrong with me'. Twice he has said that he wants to kill himself. We are terribly worried.

Dear Doctor

Martine is now 13 years old and we are concerned about her school progress. She is well behaved and does not get into any trouble at school, or at home, and this is why we have left it so long before seeking help.

Martine's reports have always been full of comments such as 'Martine needs to concentrate more'; 'Martine has good potential if she were not so easily distracted'.

Martine is a vague, dreamy sort of child. Often when you talk to her she seems to be in a world of her own. One teacher thought she may be hard of hearing, but we had this tested and her hearing is perfect.

When you give her an instruction with more than three parts, she loses track of what she has to do. Yesterday I asked her to go to her room and take the sheets off her bed and put them in the wash. Ten minutes later I went to her room to find her sitting on her bed. She genuinely did not remember what I had asked her to do.

Her memory seems so inconsistent. She can tell you in detail about what happened years ago. Last week she surprised us by recognising someone in a photo whom she had not seen for years – and telling us all about her visit to this person's house very accurately. Yet today she cannot remember the spelling list she knew yesterday.

She is terribly disorganised. She is always losing things. She has to phone her friend most afternoons to find out what homework she is supposed to do.

She is also clumsy. She is a terrible fidget – some bit of her is always squirming when she should be sitting still.

But her greatest difficulty is in concentrating on schoolwork. She sits down to her homework with the best of intentions, but she can't seem to persist with it. She is up and down at her desk and unless I sit with her nothing gets done. Even then it is a constant battle so that the whole family is upset. Getting her to complete assignments for school is impossible unless I do almost the whole thing for her. Her poor concentration is a problem at school as well. Her teachers complain that when all the other children have their eyes glued to their work, Martine is gazing out the window. Her work is often incomplete.

Martine says that she would like to become a teacher when she is an adult. We feel she is a clever girl, but if she continues like this, we can't see her achieving anything. Do you think you could help her?

David and Martine both came to see me. My assessments showed that they both had attention-deficit/hyperactivity disorder (ADHD) and they were both greatly helped by treatment for this condition.

David has the form we call the '**hyperactive-impulsive**' type of ADHD, while Martine has the form called '**inattentive**' type of ADHD*. The conditions are very different, yet they are related to one another. They are like two sides of the same coin. The profiles of the two types are outlined in Table 1.

Some children have a combination of the two types: significant difficulties with concentration *combined* with overactivity and/or impulsivity. This is known as '**combined**' type of ADHD.

**In the past, the hyperactive-impulsive form was known as 'ADHD' and the inattentive form as 'ADD' but since 1994, this terminology is no longer used. See page 17 for more about the name changes of this condition.*

Table 1 Profiles of the two types of ADHD

	Hyperactive - Impulsive type	Inattentive type
Age of onset	Early (nursery or primary school)	Later (primary or high school)
Boy to girl ratio	Boys outnumber girls	Boys and girls in equal numbers
Major difficulty	Behavior	Academic performance
Common descriptions	'Acts without thinking' 'Can't sit still'	'Quiet underachiever' 'Dreamy'

In none of the three forms is the condition the parents' fault. Rather, it results from insufficient quantities of certain chemical messengers in the child's brain. The medicines used to treat all types of ADHD act by restoring these chemical messengers to more normal levels and so enable the child to behave and learn like other children. Careful diagnosis is essential to be certain that the child's difficulties are caused by ADHD, and not by some other problem that may require a different treatment.

The diagnosis, causes, and treatment of ADHD are discussed in the following chapters.

Overview of the features of ADHD

All children with ADHD have some features of the condition; few will have all.

While some children with the hyperactive-impulsive form of ADHD will have hyperactivity *and* impulsivity, some will have only hyperactivity, while others will have only impulsivity. The hyphen between hyperactive and impulsive in this type stands for 'and/or'.

The features of all types of ADHD are listed in Table 2 and are outlined below.

It should be noted that a child *without* ADHD might have some of the features described below, but a child with ADHD experiences *significantly greater difficulties* in affected areas of development than the average child of the same age.

Table 2 Features of ADHD

Inattentive type	Hyperactive-Impulsive type	May be present in either type
Poor concentration	Impulsivity	Performance inconsistency
Task impersistence	Overactivity	Low self-esteem
Disorganization	Noisiness	Poor working memory
Forgetfulness		Poor incentival motivation
		Social clumsiness
		Learning difficulties
		Clumsiness
		Inflexibility
		Insatiability
		Defiance
		Sleep problems

Features of the inattentive type of ADHD

Poor concentration

Children with ADHD cannot concentrate with the same ease as other children of the same age. The attentional mechanisms in their brains are inefficient. This means that they have great difficulty concentrating on tedious tasks, such as school work, which greatly test these mechanisms. Their work often contains many careless errors and shows lack of precision and attention to detail.

These children have particular difficulties maintaining attention in a setting, such as a classroom, where there are many distractions. They do better in a one-to-one situation.

Children with ADHD usually have far greater difficulty concentrating on things they have to listen to than things they have to look at. They have such difficulty listening that they can appear to have a hearing problem.

In milder cases, children will be able to maintain attention for highly motivating and interactive activities, such as video games, and may be able to concentrate on tedious tasks, such as schoolwork, for short periods. However, their inefficient concentrating mechanisms soon fatigue and their attention falters. The work of such children may be full of good beginnings and poor endings. They may be able to manage relatively well in the first part of the school day, but their performance usually falls off markedly in the second half. When they return from school they may be very tired and emotionally drained from the great effort of focusing in class.

Concentrating on schoolwork may be so effortful for the child that he may be unusually reluctant to start work. Such children procrastinate far more than their peers when they have work assignments, homework, or revision to do.

Children with severe ADHD may have difficulty staying on *any* task for very long, and may be unable to sit and watch a movie or play a game they enjoy. Such children may constantly flit from one activity to another.

Poor concentration in children with ADHD is described in more detail in the next chapter.

Task impersistence

A common complaint is that children with ADHD do not complete tasks.

At home parents find that they need to supervise their children more closely than do other parents with children of the same age. Simple chores, like getting dressed in the morning, take a long time. Parents often report that 'Nothing would get done if I were not on my child's back all the time'.

These children often forget what they are asked to do. Their parents may find them staring into space, or doing something quite different.

Impersistence is a particular problem with schoolwork, as children with ADHD often do not finish their set work. They may gaze out of the window, do something else, or start disrupting other children. As they get into high school and examinations become more important, this impersistence can seriously affect academic results, as children with ADHD may not complete their examination papers within the allocated time.

Disorganization

Children with ADHD find it very difficult to follow sequences without a great deal of supervision. When such supervision is not available, they become muddled and disorganized.

Forgetfulness

'An excellent memory for what happened last year, but he cannot remember what happened yesterday', is a common description of the child with ADHD. Many know their multiplication or spelling list immediately after it has been taught, but cannot recall it the next day. Surprisingly, they often remember in great detail events that happened a long time ago.

Such children may have difficulty following an instruction with more than one part, becoming distracted or lost midway through carrying it out. They are often very absent-minded—homework is forgotten at school, pens are misplaced, and possessions lost.

Features of the hyperactive–impulsive type of ADHD

Impulsivity

Children with the impulsive type of ADHD have great difficulty stopping to think before they act (As Dennis the Menace said, 'By the time I think about it, I have done it!'). Children with this form of ADHD often do the first thing that comes into their heads; they will blurt out answers in class; they may say tactless things; they may take many risks; they have tremendous difficulty waiting their turn. They are the sort of children who may run out in front of a car without looking first.

Because of this impulsivity they do not learn from their mistakes. The problem is not necessarily that children with ADHD do not know the correct thing to do. They will often be able to explain in great detail what they should have done. They may also be quick to notice when others break the rules that they themselves do not obey. Nor is the problem that they do not want to do the right thing. They may be very upset and apologetic after the event. Their difficulty is in their lack of self-control.

The mechanisms that control behavior in the brain seem to be unreliable in the child with ADHD. ADHD is a problem of performance, not of knowledge. As Dr Russell Barclay, one of the foremost experts on this condition, put it: 'ADHD is not a matter of not knowing what to do, but of not being able to do what you know.'

Impulsivity in children with ADHD is discussed further in Chapter 3.

Overactivity

Some children with ADHD are continually on the go. They may be so restless as to seem to be 'driven by a motor'. Such a child often cannot remain seated, even for a few moments. He may wander around the classroom and the teacher may have great difficulty keeping him on his seat. Even when seated, some part of him may always be squirming.

In the past, such overactivity (also known as 'hyperactivity') was considered an essential feature of ADHD. We now know that while most children with ADHD are more fidgety or restless than other children when carefully observed, many children with ADHD are not overactive.

Even those who are very active when young may become less active than their peers as they get older—a transformation that has been described as changing from being a 'flipper' to a 'flopper' (in the sense of continually flopping down in front of the TV).

Overactivity in ADHD is discussed in Chapter 4.

Noisiness

Children with the hyperactive–impulsive type of ADHD are often boisterous and loud. They find it difficult to engage in activities quietly. Some talk excessively, driving other family members to distraction.

Some children have a habit of making all manner of repetitive noises that sound like an animal or a motor. They may be quiet for a short time if reprimanded, but the noises return, often without the child's being aware that he is making them.

Features that may be present in either type of ADHD

Performance inconsistency

All children show some inconsistency in their performance, but this is particularly marked in children with ADHD. With a tremendous amount of effort, children with ADHD can sometimes concentrate or manage to stop and think before acting like other children, but they cannot maintain this effort most of the time.

It is this performance inconsistency that has so confused observers and led to many children with ADHD being labeled as 'lazy' or 'naughty'. Those who do not understand the nature of ADHD think that because a child performs appropriately on certain occasions, he is simply not trying hard enough when he fails. In the words of one psychiatrist, 'A child with ADHD does well once and we hold that against him for the rest of his school career!'

Some situations make it easier for the child with ADHD. The child may do well with close supervision in a one-to-one setting, in a novel situation, or with someone he or she is afraid of. Even in these situations, improved performance will not last and the old difficulties resurface.

Low self-esteem

Children with ADHD are very hard on themselves. They may say negative things about themselves such as 'I am dumb'. They may cry easily and be easily offended. They may feel dissatisfied with themselves even when they succeed. For example, a child with ADHD who hit a cricket ball with great power complained that his father had bowled it too 'softly' to him. Some children with ADHD who have low self-esteem may hide this behind bravado, bragging about themselves and putting down others as a way of managing their inferiority complex.

Poor self-esteem in ADHD and the different types of behavior it may give rise to are discussed in Chapter 7.

Poor working memory

The memory difficulties of children with ADHD are not confined to the forgetfulness described earlier in this chapter. A type of short-term memory known as 'working memory' may also be impaired in children with ADHD.

The brain's working memory holds thoughts like a series of pictures pinned on a board, or a plan sketched on a note pad. These can be referred to in order to aid understanding and to guide decision-making.

A child with ADHD who has a poor working memory will experience great difficulty keeping any set of instructions or sequenced information in his mind. He will therefore find it difficult to plan ahead. He will also experience difficulty following the plot when reading a book, or even when writing a story of his own.

Many of the learning difficulties experienced by children with ADHD that affect skills such as reading comprehension, sequencing, and written expression are due to impairments in working memory.

In addition, some of the behavioral problems seen in this condition, such as lack of foresight and failure to learn from experience, are also due, in part, to problems with working memory. Poor working memory makes it difficult for the child to guide his behaviour by 'self-talk', the inner monologue that we use to keep us on track.

Poor incentival motivation

'Incentive motivation' refers to the ability to work for future rewards. As children grow older they have to defer gratification and be prepared to work for some future reward. Children with ADHD find it very difficult to sacrifice for a deferred reward. For example, they find it difficult to put in regular hours of study for something as intangible as good marks on a report card at the end of the year. They are very easily diverted from such study by the immediate gratification offered by watching TV or playing video games. This difficulty is a fundamental problem for many children with ADHD.

Social clumsiness

Children with ADHD often have difficulties reading social situations. They are often 'socially tone deaf'. They do not mean harm, but have a tendency to say very tactless things without realizing the effect they are having. They seem to have difficulty predicting the consequences of their actions and responding appropriately to the occasion. They may 'come on too strong'. These children often do not pick up the same cues as other children of the same age. They often do not read facial expressions and may be oblivious to whether someone is angry or upset with them. Because they fail to develop the same degree of reserve as normal children, they may behave in front of others in ways that are not appropriate for children their age.

Although such abnormal behavior may be apparent to all who meet the child, the people who are most likely to notice are the child's peers. With them, the child with ADHD often sticks out like a sore thumb. Typically such children have little or no insight into how differently they are perceived. They do not seem to be able to learn the skills that are required to mix with others. They often become loners, or play with children younger or older than themselves. With younger children, they blend in because of their immaturity. With older children, more allowances are made for their inappropriate behavior.

Social clumsiness in children with ADHD is further described in Chapter 8.

Learning difficulties

All children with ADHD under-achieve academically. Most children with ADHD will have difficulties in primary school with skills such as reading, spelling, and mathematics. Many have very untidy handwriting.

Other common areas of difficulty are in reading comprehension and written expression.

Some children with mild ADHD may do well during primary school. However, during high school such children often start to fall behind, as greater skills in concentration and organization are required.

Learning difficulties in ADHD are described in Chapter 5.

Clumsiness

While some children with ADHD are excellent athletes, most are poorly coordinated. Catching a small ball and writing neatly are skills which many children with ADHD find extremely difficult. Many have low muscle tone (slight floppiness) when younger and have a poorly co-ordinated running style.

Inflexibility

Children with ADHD are often very literal, and 'black and white' in their understanding of the world around them. They find it difficult to compromise. As a result parents often find themselves in conflict with their child over many issues.

'Every discussion is an argument' is a phrase parents often use to describe their child's behavior. Once the child with ADHD takes up an attitude to something, it is often almost impossible to get him or her to change. Children with ADHD may become very fixated on certain rules and follow these rigidly. They have difficulty understanding when such rules can be reasonably bent.

Insatiability

Children with ADHD may be insatiable in their activities; not knowing when to stop, the way another child of their age would. This may be seen when they become overexcited in play and cannot calm down again when it is time to be serious. Instead they become more and more excited and non-compliant. They may even become excessively defiant and provocative despite reasonable requests to calm down.

They may show their insatiability by never being satisfied with any treat and in nagging for more and more things they want. This difficulty is related to problems that these children have with delaying gratification—they find it very difficult to wait for a reward or treat. Many parents find this insatiability the hardest part of ADHD to manage; they are worn down by their child's constant nagging which can last for hours, or even days, on end.

Defiant behavior

Many children with ADHD, particularly those with the hyperactive-impulsive type, have great difficulty obeying reasonable rules and regulations. When asked to do something by an authority figure, they may refuse or even become abusive. Punishment often does not help. Children with ADHD with defiant behavior are very hard to discipline. As they get older they may get into problems with stealing, fire lighting, and other anti-social behavior.

Defiant behavior is described further in Chapter 6.

Sleep problems

Many children with ADHD have difficulty falling asleep and are up until late at night. Once asleep they may be very restless—their beds often look like a battlefield the next morning. Others may so exhaust themselves with their overactivity during the day that they fall asleep and sleep very soundly. Many children with ADHD persist with bed-wetting later than other children. Night terrors, sleepwalking, and bed-wetting are all more common in children with ADHD.

Associated (co-morbid) conditions

There are a number of conditions that are more common in individuals with ADHD than in the general population. The tendency of a condition to co-exist with another is known as 'co-morbidity'. This comes from the medical term, 'morbidity', that relates to the proportion of people *having* a particular disorder (not to be confused with the term 'mortality', which refers to the proportion of people *dying* from a condition).

The co-morbid conditions associated with ADHD are listed in Table 3.

Figure 1 demonstrates how different conditions often co-exist. For example, a child with ADHD can have anxiety and conduct disorder in addition to ADHD. From the percentages shown in the figure it should be noted that, while these conditions are more common in individuals with ADHD, most individuals with ADHD will not develop a co-morbid condition.

Table 3 Co-morbidity: conditions that are more common in individuals with ADHD

Tic disorder
Dyslexia
Oppositional disorder
Conduct disorder
Asperger syndrome
Depression
Anxiety disorder
Obsessive compulsive disorder
Bipolar disorder

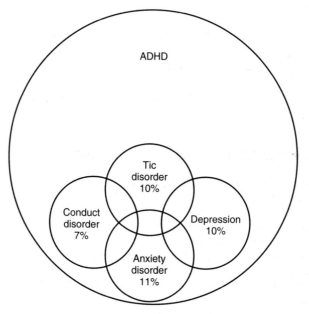

Figure 1 ADHD and some of its co-morbid conditions. Each circle represents those individuals with a particular disorder. Overlapping areas show how a number of conditions often coexist in individuals with ADHD.

Parents who have a child with ADHD who has a particular co-morbid condition can find out more about the disorder by referring to the relevant section of this book. Tic disorder is discussed in Section 2 of Chapter 4. Dyslexia is described in Chapter 5. Oppositional disorder and conduct disorder are described in Chapter 6. A description of Asperger syndrome can be found at the end of Chapter 8. Depression, anxiety disorder, obsessive compulsive disorder, and bipolar disorder are dealt with in Chapter 9. The reason why co-morbid disorders occur more commonly in individuals with ADHD is discussed in Chapter 10.

How common is ADHD?

ADHD is one of the most common conditions in childhood, affecting as many as 5% of school-aged children. It affects about three times as many boys as girls and occurs in all ethnic groups.

It seems that the predominance of boys in the overall number is due to their overrepresentation in the hyperactive-impulsive group. In the inattentive group, there are as many affected girls as boys.

The hyperactive-impulsive type is three times more common in boys in the community yet many clinics see six times as many boys with this type. It seems that boys with the hyperactive-impulsive type are far more likely to be noticed than girls with this type. Despite the predominance of boys, the hyperactive-impulsive type can be just as severe in an affected girl as in a boy.

When does ADHD start?

Although the difficulties in both types of ADHD are present from birth, problems generally do not become apparent until later in childhood.

In children with the hyperactive-impulsive type, the behavioral problems are often apparent from infancy. Such children are generally difficult babies and active, challenging toddlers. The child's teacher may complain that he is not managing in the classroom and playground from the earliest school years.

In children with a milder form of this type of ADHD, the child may manage in primary school without much difficulty but, with the onset of puberty and the greater demands of high school, problems often emerge.

Children with the inattentive type of ADHD generally experience difficulties with schoolwork when the work becomes more demanding.

While some do develop reading and writing delays in primary school, many manage well until late primary or early high school. High school requires skills in self-organization, sustained concentration, proficient written expression, and self-direction that these children often do not possess.

Historical background

ADHD is not a new condition. The first description of children with the disorder was by an English physician, Dr George Still, in 1902. He described 20 children in his practice with impaired concentration and overactivity. He recognized that this was not due to any fault in their upbringing. Dr Still did not give the condition a name.

Interest in the condition was rekindled after an encephalitis epidemic in the USA in 1917–18. Many children acquired a form of encephalitis that left them with attention difficulties, overactivity, and impulsivity. In such children, the encephalitis virus had damaged parts of the brain that are impaired in children with ADHD, and hence their problems were similar.

Since that time, ADHD has become the most studied developmental disorder in childhood. A number of name changes attest to the rapid evolution in our understanding of this condition.

In the 1950s attention was focused on children with hyperactivity and the term 'hyperkinetic – impulse disorder' was used. In the 1960s the term 'minimal brain dysfunction' was widely used for children with ADHD.

In the sixties, attitudes to ADHD in the UK and the USA began to diverge. In the UK and other parts of Europe, the International Classification of Diseases of the World Health Organization was followed. At that time, this classification recognized only children with 'hyperkinetic disorder', a term applied to children with severe overactivity.

In North America a different classification of disorders, the Diagnostic and Statistical Manual of the American Psychiatric Association, was followed. In the US, largely due to the work of the Canadian psychologist, Virginia Douglas, impairment in concentration (i.e. attention), rather than overactivity, was seen as the fundamental deficit in this disorder. The term 'attention deficit disorder' (ADD) was then introduced in the US for the condition. Both children with and without hyperactivity were recognized as having ADD.

Those with hyperactivity were considered to have ADD+H while those without were considered to have ADD−H.

In the late eighties the term 'ADHD' was introduced in the US to describe those with the hyperactivity and/or impulsivity, while the term 'ADD' was reserved for those with poor concentration alone.

Since 1994 in the US, the term 'attention-deficit/hyperactivity disorder' (abbreviated to either 'AD/HD' or 'ADHD') has been used to encompass the spectrum of children with *all* forms of the condition. The three subtypes 'inattentive', 'hyperactive-impulsive', and 'combined' were introduced at this time. It is this terminology, with the simpler abbreviation 'ADHD' rather than 'AD/HD' that is followed in this book.

Over the past decade, attitudes to diagnosis and treatment in the UK and the rest of Europe have increasingly followed those in the USA. The 1990 update of the International Classification of Diseases (ICD-10) and the 1994 update of the Diagnostic and Statistical Manual of the American Psychiatric Association (DSM-IV) were very similar in their criteria for diagnosis of the condition.

Further landmarks in this convergence of views included the recommendations published by the National Institute of Clinical Excellence (NICE) in the UK in November 2000 and the International Consensus Statement on ADHD published in January 2002. The role of NICE is to provide patients, health professionals, and the public with 'authoritative, robust, and reliable guidance' on current best practice in health issues. Their approach was consistent with US practice. The International Consensus Statement was issued by over 90 of the world's leading scientists, researchers, and clinicians treating ADHD from 12 countries including the USA and the UK. It reflected the unanimity of views across the Atlantic.

All English-speaking countries now use the same terminology, criteria for diagnosis, and treatment protocols. No matter where they live, children with ADHD and their families benefit from the huge amount of research undertaken in centres all over the world, as well as from the wide range of literature, videos, and equipment directed at helping parents and teachers assist children with ADHD.

With the realisation that a proportion of children with ADHD continue to have difficulties throughout adulthood, an increasing amount of research and support is now also being directed to residual ADHD in adults.

Section 2

Some characteristic difficulties

2 Poor concentration

'Peter must pay attention.' 'Peter is too easily distracted in class.' 'Peter must take care not to be so careless.' These are the comments that keep recurring in our son's report cards from year to year. It has always been difficult to get Peter to concentrate on schoolwork. His mind always seems to be elsewhere. When he does attend, he is soon distracted. Getting him to do his homework is a constant battle. Last year I was finding it so stressful, that I decided not to get involved with his homework at all. As a result, Peter spent many afternoons on detention. Unfortunately, this did not seem to help.

Peter's distracted state means that he often does not hear what the teacher is saying. He often loses notes that he should bring home.

He has trouble carrying out instructions at home too. If I ask him to do something he gets distracted midway through, or forgets what I asked him to do.

He is terribly disorganized. I have to organize and supervise him in everything. If I did not keep tabs on everything he needs to do for school he would never succeed. In the last three weeks he has lost his glasses, his school diary, and his lunch box.

The perplexing thing is that Peter can concentrate very well when something interests him. He can spend hours totally fixated on a video game. When I pointed this out to my family doctor he thought that it meant that Peter did not have ADHD. But the assessment by the pediatrician and psychologist showed that Peter does have ADHD and the effect of the medicine has been remarkable.

Poor concentration in children with ADHD

Children with ADHD often have difficulty giving close attention to details. As a result they make careless mistakes in their schoolwork. They often do not follow through on instructions and fail to finish schoolwork, chores, and other duties. Children with ADHD are very easily distracted, particularly in a group setting. They tend to be forgetful in daily activities. Their difficulties seem to be greater for concentration on things they have to listen to (auditory attention) than things they have to look at (visual attention).

To understand the difficulties that children with ADHD face we must first understand the attentional process in the brain.

The attentional process in the brain

When we look at something, a great deal of information about everything in our field of vision travels from our eyes to the brain. This picture of our whole visual field is known as the *visual buffer*. Our brain is able to select a portion of this information to focus on. This portion selected for attention is called the *attentional window*.

The attentional window can be shifted voluntarily from one part of the visual buffer to another. Not only can it change its location, but it can also expand or shrink its scope, like a zoom lens. That is, from all the visual information entering the brain, we select what we will pay attention to and how closely we will pay attention, and we can change this at will. With an efficient attentional mechanism in the brain, the attentional window can be focused on one part of the visual buffer for long periods of time.

The efficiency with which attention can be sustained increases as children grow older.

A younger child's attention will wander unless the material in the attentional window is very interesting and the information in the rest of the visual buffer is relatively boring. Even then, the attentional mechanism quickly tires and attention cannot be sustained for long.

There is a comparable attentional mechanism for listening. The *auditory buffer* contains all the sounds heard at a particular time. The *auditory attention window* focuses on one particular source of sound, in the way a radio tunes into one particular frequency. Selecting part of the buffer and sustaining attention on one part of it is generally more difficult for auditory than for visual stimuli, as listening is generally harder than looking. This is especially so for children with ADHD.

Difficult tasks for attentional mechanisms

Although children with ADHD have inefficient attentional mechanisms that quickly tire, it is wrong to believe that children with

ADHD cannot concentrate at all. Their mechanisms for concentrating are inefficient and unreliable, not absent. It is this that makes their performance so inconsistent.

Having an immature concentrating mechanism is like having a weak leg that allows one to walk for short bursts, but does not allow one to keep up with one's peers for long stretches. Children with ADHD are easily fatigued when their attention needs to be sustained.

Attentional mechanisms are more stressed under certain circumstances than others, and it is in the difficult situations that children with ADHD are most likely to find that their attentional mechanisms are failing.

Tedious tasks are very difficult for immature attentional mechanisms. This is why younger children cannot be expected to concentrate on tedious tasks. Unfortunately much of the work that school children need to perform is very tedious and children with ADHD quickly become distracted. It is not that a normal child finds the work any more interesting than the child with ADHD, it is just that the normal child finds concentrating easier.

The attentional difficulties may give children with ADHD an unfocused appearance. Common descriptions include 'vague', 'dreamy', and having 'glazed eyes'.

Children with ADHD tire easily when having to concentrate, so their work may be full of good beginnings that then peter out. Often their schoolwork will be much better in the morning when they are fresher and better able to compensate for their attentional difficulties. This may be true for all children, but for those with ADHD the contrast will be greater.

If the task is long or arduous, children with ADHD quickly lose concentration. This is why they are so often described as being impersistent. This is further compounded by their difficulty in working for a distant reward—their lack of incentival motivation.

Difficulties with concentration also result in children with ADHD often being confused and unable to understand instructions. When the child with ADHD has to listen, he has difficulty remaining tuned to the 'right station'. His concentration is easily distracted onto other sounds and so he hears only parts of the instruction. No wonder parents say that their instructions go in one ear and out the other. These difficulties may be compounded by the problems with short-term memory and language comprehension that frequently occur in children with ADHD.

A common observation made about the visual attention of children with ADHD is that they may seem to 'see everything at a glance'. Because of their difficulty with sustained attention, they may become reliant on a quick appraisal of any new situation. They may, therefore, surprise parents and teachers by how much they can take in with seemingly little effort. However, they have difficulty absorbing more than the superficial features.

Children with ADHD tend to flit from one thing to another. Parents often notice how poor such children are at occupying themselves. Having moved quickly from one toy, or activity, to another, they quickly lose concentration and can then become aimless. It is at times like these that their behavior may become attention seeking, or that they may get into mischief.

Another difficulty for children with ADHD is in adjusting their level of attention to suit the situation. For example, children may be less focused in the playground and then need to become more attentive when they return to the classroom after recess. Children with ADHD have great difficulty coping with such transitions. Instead of increasing their state of alertness once in the classroom, like other children of the same age, they remain unfocused and do not settle back to work again.

Children with ADHD have their greatest difficulty sustaining concentration if there are many distractions. The usual classroom is full of distractions because of the presence of so many other children, and children with ADHD are at their worst in such an environment. By contrast, they are at their most attentive and learn best in a one-to-one setting.

Sometimes a small group of children with ADHD is withdrawn from the large classroom for special help, in the hope that they will do better with fewer distractions. However, this environment is likely to be very distracting because children with ADHD usually distract one another. Whenever possible, children with ADHD should not be grouped together in a class.

Children with ADHD will concentrate best if they are receiving frequent positive feedback. They usually manage best if the work is very interesting and if there are immediate consequences for their actions.

Their concentration is usually at its best early in the day and diminishes as their attentional mechanisms fatigue. Parents and teachers are advised to arrange for demanding work to be done in the first part of the day, and to make some allowance for reduced concentration as the day progresses.

Noisiness and attention in ADHD

A tendency to be noisy, whether at work or play, is a general characteristic of children with the hyperactive-impulsive type of ADHD. Research has shown that as children with ADHD concentrate intently, they tend to become noisier. This tendency applies even to those who are not particularly noisy at other times.

It seems as if many children with ADHD need to provide some constant noise and self-talk to help them block out distractions and to focus on a task. A teacher who believes the child is becoming noisier because she is not working, rather than because she is working, can easily misinterpret this. Allowances should be made for such involuntary noisiness that accompanies productive work.

3
Impulsivity

Impulsivity, the difficulty in being able to think before acting, causes many problems for children with ADHD both at home and at school. Teaching the child to consider the consequences of an action does not solve the problem of impulsivity in a child with ADHD. Children with this condition lack the reflective and behavioral inhibition mechanisms needed to apply such teaching to their everyday lives.

Behavioral inhibition mechanisms in the brain

Normal preschool children are impulsive creatures. If they see something they want, they usually cannot resist the temptation to take it. If they do not like something, they act out their aggression or frustration without any thought of the consequences. We regard this as normal behavior at this age.

Jeffrey A. Gray first proposed the theory that certain structures in the frontal part of the brain act as a behavioral inhibition system (BIS) to control behavior. Gray's theory was based on work with rat brains, but identical structures exist in the human brain. Some authorities believe that the reason very young children are so impulsive is that their brain BIS is not yet active. Their behavior is like a simple reflex arc, like a knee jerk reaction.

As the frontal lobe of the brain develops, the nerve cells (neurones) that control behavior become more powerful and start playing a mediating role between the input and output of the brain. This allows the individual to stop and think before acting. Only then can the knowledge and experience that the child has acquired play a role in preventing impulsive responses.

Children with ADHD who behave in an impulsive way do not do so because of ignorance. They usually know as well as other children of their age what they should and should not do. However, they respond in a reflexive (impulsive) way to the things that happen around them. If one observes the behavior of children with ADHD with this in mind, their repeated misdemeanors and failure to 'learn' from their mistakes, and from punishment, is understandable.

Telling a child with ADHD to 'stop and think' is often asking the impossible. It would be analogous to asking an adult not to put out a hand to break a fall. The knowledge that one is going to fall on something soft does not allow one to inhibit the reflex action of stretching out one's hands. Similarly, knowledge is not enough to stop the child with ADHD from behaving impulsively. It is only when behavior inhibition systems start to become active, either as a result of normal brain maturation, or by being 'switched on' by medication (as will be discussed in Chapter 15), that the child with ADHD is able to stop and think before acting.

Manifestations of impulsivity

The impulsivity of children with ADHD manifests itself in many ways. They act impulsively, think impulsively, and feel things impulsively.

Most obvious is the tendency to act without thinking. This may mean that the child endangers himself or others by risk-taking acts. It also means that the child is likely to make heedless or careless errors because of his failure to think carefully.

Children with ADHD will sometimes act on a whim or with minimal encouragement, especially from another child, and other children will take advantage of this. Children with ADHD are often 'set up' by other children to do things that the other children recognize as dangerous. Their difficulties are further compounded because they generally lack the guile not to get caught. Often a child with ADHD will join in with a number of other children in carrying out some misdemeanor, and only the child with ADHD will be caught. A further disadvantage is that the child with ADHD, having gained a reputation for foolhardy behavior, is often blamed for a misdemeanour whether guilty or not.

Because they take risks, children with the impulsive type of ADHD are very accident-prone. It is not uncommon for children with this form of ADHD to have broken a number of bones during their childhood.

Accidental poisoning and burning are also more common in this group of children.

Children with ADHD are often compulsively destructive. They are quick to damage or destroy toys. Parents are often puzzled because their child may destroy toys that he enjoys. They do not seem to be able to control this behavior. Their impulsivity also means that they are generally harder on their toys and are more likely to damage their parents' property and the property of others.

It is extremely difficult for an impulsive child to wait in line when queuing is needed. He is also likely to blurt out in class and to find it very difficult to wait his turn in a game or other activity. Children with ADHD often provide answers that show that they have not listened carefully to the question.

Children who are impulsive quickly learn to take short cuts in the way in which they do things. They want to finish things very quickly and will find all kinds of ways of getting to the end of an activity without worrying about the quality of what they produce.

Impulsivity gets in the way of delaying gratification, and children with this difficulty find it almost impossible to work for a long-term goal. They are reward-driven like other children, but need that reward immediately. Parents will find that if a treat is promised, children with ADHD will nag incessantly while waiting for it. Parents often learn not to tell their child about treats and outings because they want to avoid the constant nagging that goes on until the reward or treat is given, and because these children over-react should the outing or treat not occur.

Children with ADHD often cannot stop themselves from touching things or people. Other children of the same age may respond very badly to this touching. Parents often complain that children with ADHD cannot keep their hands to themselves. The habit of touching things can be very embarrassing to the parents when they take their child out, and things may get broken when the child is visiting or shopping.

Impulsive thinking makes children with ADHD very illogical at times. Instead of thinking about things in a clear sequence, they move impulsively from one idea to another. It is very difficult to reason with a child who thinks in this way.

Situations or games requiring sharing, cooperation, and restraint with peers are particularly problematical. Group situations are particularly difficult for children with ADHD, because it is in such situations that the individual's impulsivity must be subjugated to the needs of the whole group.

A tendency toward impulsivity interferes with a child's ability to carry out sequential tasks, that is, the ability to get things into the right order. Children with significant difficulty in sequential organization will experience problems with tasks such as following directions, counting, telling time, using a calendar, and getting to know the day's schedule. Such a child will often have difficulty getting dressed quickly, having the correct books ready for a class, getting to the right classroom, and following complex instructions. It may also result in spelling errors such as 'hegde' for 'hedge' and 'fisrt' for 'first'.

This is why children with ADHD often benefit from having a set routine, and are at their best in a structured situation where their impulsivity is contained. A regular course of events helps a child anticipate the next activity and remember the schedule.

Emotional impulsivity results in quick changes of mood. Children show this by having 'a short fuse' and a low frustration tolerance. Parents will notice that the child seems to be managing quite well and then suddenly becomes upset for no apparent reason.

Children with impulsive ADHD may have difficulty controlling their tendency to be noisy. Generally they are boisterous children who are more talkative than their peers.

Management of impulsivity

Cognitive therapy, a form of therapy that aims to teach children self-control, has generally shown disappointing results in children with ADHD. However, it is worth trying this form of therapy in a motivated and insightful child as he may be able to develop a greater ability to stop and think before acting.

In contrast to the generally disappointing results with cognitive therapy, medication usually plays a very dramatic role in controlling impulsivity. In many children medicine alone is enough to ameliorate this difficulty.

Parents, teachers, and others who come into contact with the child with ADHD need to understand that impulsive behavior is not completely under the child's control. Wherever possible, allowances should be made for this. Environmental changes and modification of goals are important ways of helping the child. For example, parents should ensure that children with ADHD who take risks because of their impulsivity are properly supervised in potentially dangerous situations. Matches, sharp knives, and other potentially dangerous implements may need to be kept out of the child's reach.

Short-term, easily obtainable goals may need to be set. For example, it may be unrealistic to punish an impulsive child with ADHD every time he calls out an answer in class. It may be more appropriate to set him the goal of not more than one such outburst per lesson. The child should be praised if he successfully limits his behavior in this way.

4
Excessive movement

This chapter describes two quite different types of excessive movement that may occur in a child with ADHD.

The first is the hyperactivity (overactivity) that occurs as part of the condition in some, but by no means all, children with the disorder. This is described in the first section of this chapter.

The second type of excessive movement is a motor tic disorder (a motor tic is a type of sudden, repetitive movement). Tics are more common in children with ADHD. They are described in the second section of this chapter.

Section 1   Hyperactivity

Greg was overactive even before he was born. When I was pregnant with him, I often could not get to sleep at night because he used to kick so much. He was fine as a young baby, but from about nine months, when he first learned to walk, he became a handful. We used the same cot for all four children, but only Greg was able to climb out by the time he was one year old. He would climb up onto tables, chairs, anywhere he could. He had no sense of danger. He seemed not to feel pain. He would fall down and simply get back up again. He did not understand the word 'No!'. He had to be watched every minute.

By the end of the day I was exhausted with continually supervising him. Then the battle would start to try to get him to sleep. He would still be up at midnight; his older brothers and his sister would be fast asleep by about 8.30. He could not be kept in his bedroom and would come into the lounge. He would be tired and unreasonable and climb all over my husband and me, but we could not get him to stay in bed.

He started at preschool when he was three and a half and the teacher complained that he was aggressive toward the other children. He also would not sit down during story-time or stay on his mattress during rest time. A special assistant was employed by the preschool to help Greg cope and things seemed to settle down.

When Greg was due to start school at five, the preschool teacher suggested that he was not mature enough and should stay on at the preschool for another year. During that year he settled down quite a lot and we thought he was ready for school.

The first year of proper school was a disaster for Greg. He spent most of the time being punished for getting out of his seat, for calling out, and for disrupting the other children. The other children called him a 'Naughty Greg' and he became more and more discouraged and defiant. He did not seem to be learning anything at school at all. He was always in trouble, and seemed to be blamed for everything, even though it sometimes was not his fault. At the end of the year the teacher told me that if she had to teach Greg for another year she would have resigned!

At the end of the first week of his second year at school, his new teacher sent a note home asking to see me. She said that Greg was impossible to teach. She suggested we take Greg to a pediatrician for an assessment because he seemed hyperactive and may need medication. This was the first time that medicine was suggested.

We had the assessment that showed that Greg was a very intelligent boy, but that he had ADHD. We had never heard of this condition before. We read everything we could about the condition and after satisfying ourselves that the medication was perfectly safe, Greg was started on Ritalin [methylphenidate]. The change in his behavior and mood was miraculous. One hour after the tablet I had my first proper conversation with Greg. For the first time in his life he was able to sit still and look at a book. He was able to sit down at mealtimes like the other children.

The teacher reported a wonderful change in Greg at school. All of a sudden his reading came along and his whole attitude to life changed. The other children started to be more positive about him and he was invited to his first birthday party.

Now 5 years later, Greg still takes Ritalin every day. If he forgets a tablet he gets into trouble at school because of his behavior. He calls them his 'thinking tablets' and they have made all the difference to his life and ours.

Temporary immobilization—a developmental skill

If one visits a preschool and observes a group of 3 year olds, and then visits a primary school and observes a group of 8 year olds, one notices an important difference: the 3 year olds are more restless and fidgety than the 8 year olds.

Filming of children of different ages shows that the level of activity in normal children decreases markedly in the first 3 years of life and then, more gradually, over the rest of the school years.

This is most likely to be due to the greater influence, with increasing age, of inhibiting mechanisms in the brain that temporarily immobilize parts of the body when they are not needed. Young children cannot efficiently immobilize muscles in this way and associated movements of their bodies, such as 'mirror' movements and overflow movements, are common. 'Mirror' movements occur when a child does something with one side of the body and another side moves in unison. Younger children also have more 'overflow' movements, a tendency for some part of the body to move when the child is excited or concentrating (e.g. moving the tongue while writing).

The persistence of immaturities of motor function, such as mirror and overflow movements, constitute part of the 'soft' neurological signs that are common in children with ADHD of all ages and provide evidence of immaturity of parts of the brain that control movement in these children.

Many children with ADHD continue to have a degree of muscular overactivity that indicates that movement inhibiting mechanisms in the brain do not seem to be as mature as they should be.

These movement inhibition mechanisms are not under voluntary control, although with great effort a child can temporarily over-ride them. This cannot be sustained for long, however. Asking a child with ADHD and hyperactivity to sit still is asking the impossible.

Varying degrees of overactivity

No aspect of ADHD has caused more confusion than that of overactivity. As discussed in the first chapter, ADHD used to be called 'hyperactivity'. This meant that unless overactivity was present, the diagnosis was not made. However, we now know that overactivity may be so mild as to go unnoticed in children with the disorder.

The degree of overactivity of children with ADHD varies from the child with nothing more than excessive feelings of restlessness, to the child who is almost never still.

There are no instruments that reliably measure activity levels, but three descriptive categories of overactivity are usually recognized:

Restless feeling

Many children with ADHD are not unusually active for their age, but simply complain of feelings of restlessness.

'Fidgets

A child with the 'fidgets' may be described as 'a can of worms', 'a rocker', 'a jiggler', 'a wriggler', or 'a squirmer'. These children may squirm their bodies when they are seated. They may fidget with their hands, for example by drumming on the table or fiddling with things on their desk.

'Runners and climbers'

Children with ADHD who have the more severe form of overactivity are often described as 'being driven by a motor'. Such children are almost never still. They run instead of walking. They do not like to be restricted in any way. If held, they usually try to wriggle free. They will clamber over objects and climb onto things when other children of their age no longer do such things.

Such behavior often leads to repeated falls and injuries such as bruises, cuts, and grazes. This is particularly the case because children with ADHD often have a poor sense of danger, are impulsive, and learn poorly from experience.

When children with this sort of overactivity level become tired, their activity level may increase rather than decrease, making it difficult for them to fall asleep.

Underactivity in older children with ADHD

Most overactive children with ADHD become less active as they get older. Some remain 'outdoor' children who much prefer being active to sitting still. Some may develop normal levels of activity as adolescents.

Other children with ADHD may become less active than their non-ADHD peers in adolescence. These children become reluctant to take part in physical activities. They prefer to spend time in front of the television or video game. Such 'couch potatoes' run the risk of becoming obese from eating inappropriately for their activity level.

Section 2   Tic disorders

A tic is a sudden, repetitive movement or vocalization (production of a sound). The movement may occur in any part of the body. The sound may range from a meaningless grunt to a short phrase.

Motor tics

A motor tic consists of a repeated movement.

Simple motor tics consist of brief sudden movements and include eye blinking, neck jerking, shoulder shrugging, facial grimacing, and mouth opening.

Complex motor tics are distinct, coordinated patterns of successive movements involving several muscle groups and include grooming behaviors (such as arranging the hair), jumping, stamping, and smelling an object.

Vocal tics

A vocal tic consists of a repeated sound or vocalization.

Simple vocal tics include throat clearing, grunting, sniffing, barking, and snorting.

Complex vocal tics include repetition of single words or phrases (out of context). If the word or phrase is rude this is known as *coprolalia*. If the child repeats his own words this is known as *palilalia*. If he repeats the last word he has heard another person speak this is known as *echolalia*. Coprolalia, palilalia, and echolalia are all very rare.

The cause of tics

Tics come about because of a genetically determined over-sensitivity (*hyper-reactivity*) of certain brain cells that control muscular movement and sound production. In children who inherit a predisposition to tics, these cells become oversensitive to certain normal brain chemicals (neurotransmitters) that transmit impulses from one nerve cell to the next. It is this over-sensitivity that gives muscles a tendency to be 'twitchy' and the speech center a tendency to 'misfire'.

Will the tics go away?

Tics may begin at any age after infancy. Once they appear they come and go, often for no discernable reason.

The nature of the tic may change over time, and more than one tic may be present at one time.

In a small number of children, the tics may become significantly worse for a period. During such a 'tic crisis', tics become more widespread and the movements and vocalizations more marked. A tic crisis usually resolves spontaneously after days or weeks.

Most individuals grow out of their tics at puberty.

The link between ADHD and tics

Tics are more common in individuals with ADHD: they occur in approximately 10% of those with the condition. Nearly all children with *severe* tics will have ADHD.

This association (co-morbidity) occurs because tics and ADHD share a number of causative genes. This is described further in Chapter 10.

Tic triggers

Tics may be triggered or exacerbated by emotional stresses such as anxiety or fatigue. Stress may aggravate tics, often in a cyclical way: stress increases tics, but tics also increase stress because they embarrass the child.

Tics are sometimes referred to as 'nervous habits' but, while a tic may become more prominent when the child becomes self-conscious or emotionally stressed, it is not actually caused by anxiety—only made worse by it.

Tics are occasionally triggered by some physical condition that causes discomfort to the affected part of the body. For example, a child may acquire an eye infection and then start blinking. The blinking continues after the original trigger has resolved. Sometimes parents will seek many opinions and try many treatments under the misconception that the tic is caused by a physical disorder in the affected part of the body (e.g. that a coughing tic is due to asthma). Such treatments will prove fruitless if the movement is a tic.

ADHD medication and tics

The two main medicines used in ADHD, methylphenidate (Ritalin) and dexamphetamine, can trigger a tic in susceptible children. They can also worsen a tic that has already appeared.

It must be emphasized that in most children with ADHD these medicines have no effect on tics, and in some children tics actually improve when one of these medicines is given.

Research reported in 1999 indicated that when children with ADHD who received one of these medicines were compared over the span of several years to children who had not, the proportion in whom tics ultimately appeared was not statistically different. Similarly, the proportion in whom tics ultimately resolved was also no different. This has lead most doctors to accept that, while these medicines may cause a tic to appear earlier than it otherwise would have, such a tic would eventually have appeared even if the child had not taken the medicine. Furthermore, these medicines do not seem to affect the chance of the tics eventually resolving.

In the light of these findings, children with ADHD who have tics can be given these medicines if required. If tics worsen, the medicine should be stopped to check whether the tics then improve. If they do, it is necessary to re-start the medicine for a short time to observe whether the tics reappear. This last step is important because tics so often improve for no discernable reason that the improvement may have been incidental and not connected with stopping the medicine.

If re-introducing the medicine a second time does cause the tics to worsen, it is best to try an alternative medicine. If a suitable alternative medicine cannot be found, a decision must be made as to whether the improvement in the child's ADHD symptoms justifies worsening of the tics. In some children the positive effects of the medication on the child's mood and learning justifies continuing with the medicine, in others it does not.

Types of tic disorder

Tic disorders are classified according to duration of the condition, and whether both motor and vocal tics are present. It should be noted that this classification is based on how long the tics have been present *in the past*. We have no way of knowing whether or when a child with tics will grow out of this tendency. Referring to the condition by one of the following four terms, therefore, does not imply any knowledge about how long the tics will persist *in the future*.

Transient tics

The term 'transient tic disorder' is appropriate if motor and/or vocal tics have been present for more than 4 months but less than 12 months. Transient tics are common.

If the tics persist for more than 12 months, the disorder is no longer regarded as 'transient' and one of the following three terms is then used:

Chronic motor tics

This term is used if one or more motor tics have been present for more than 12 months. This term is only appropriate if there are no vocal tics present.

Chronic vocal tics

The term is used if one or more vocal tics have been present for more than 12 months. This term is only appropriate if there are no motor tics present.

Tourette disorder

The term 'Tourette disorder' (or the synonym, 'Tourette syndrome') is appropriate if there are multiple motor tics *and* one or more vocal tics that have been present for over 12 months. The name of the disorder honors the French neurologist, Dr George de la Tourette, who first reported the condition in 1825.

Tourette disorder has often been inaccurately portrayed on the television and in movies. This has led to a misconception that individuals with the disorder often display unusual features such as coprolalia (a vocal tic involving socially unacceptable, often obscene, words) and echokinesis (a complex motor tic involving imitation of someone else's movements). There has also been a tendency to portray individuals with the disorder as if an unusual temperament and limited abilities were part of the condition. In fact coprolalia and echokinesis are extremely rare in Tourette disorder and most individuals with the disorder have a normal temperament and are of average ability. The vast majority of individuals with Tourette disorder have a mild form of the condition.

A proper use of the term Tourette disorder is based on the *past* pattern and duration of the tics. The diagnosis of Tourette disorder does not imply that the tics will persist throughout the individual's lifespan. Many children with the condition will grow out of their tics at puberty.

Emotional problems may arise in individuals with Tourette disorder because of the adverse effects of the tics on the individual's self-esteem. They may also be manifestations of one of the co-morbid conditions that Tourette disorder shares with ADHD. The myth of a 'Tourette temperament' is probably based on these associated, co-morbid emotional disorders. Characteristics wrongly attributed to Tourette disorder itself include impulsivity (part of associated ADHD), inflexibility (part of associated obsessive-compulsive disorder), and learning difficulty (part of associated dyslexia). Such characteristics are not an intrinsic part of Tourette disorder, which is essentially a disorder of movement. Any associated behavioral problem in an individual with Tourette disorder should be regarded as a separate problem to be treated on its own merits.

Treatment of tics

Since tics are often made worse by self-consciousness and stress, it is important to try to ignore a child's tics. Adverse comments and reminders to stop the tics will usually make them worse.

A child with tics may be able to voluntarily suppress her tics in certain situations, but such self-control should not be taken for granted, as it is usually impossible for a child to sustain this.

Some children with tics benefit from learning stress-reduction techniques. Cognitive therapy (mind-over-matter) training is also helpful for some children. A child may also be taught techniques to cover up her tics and to deal with the questions and comments of others.

Teachers will need to have the tics explained to them as both motor and vocal tics may be misinterpreted as rude or disruptive within the classroom and the child punished for something she cannot control.

A sudden motor tic while carrying out certain activities may put a child and those around her at risk and so activities such as carrying hot fluids or learning to drive will have to be curtailed for some children with tics. If tics persist into late high school, the choice of vocational training will also need to take into account the effect of the individual's tics in the workplace. For example, training to be a cook would be inappropriate if a sudden movement in a kitchen while handling hot fluids could put the individual and her workmates at risk. Similarly a career as a hairdresser would be inappropriate if a sudden movement of the hand could place a prospective client in danger.

There are a number of medicines that can reduce tics by affecting brain chemicals (neurotransmitters). These can be very effective in some children and may eradicate tics completely. The most common medicines used for this purpose are clonidine and risperidone. These medicines are discussed further in Chapter 16.

5 Learning difficulties

A child with ADHD may underachieve at school for a variety of reasons. Learning difficulties may occur both in children with and without behavior problems. Even when behavior problems are present, the learning difficulty may be related more to impairment in information processing than the behavior problem.

Specific deficits in information processing in the brain are the commonest causes of academic difficulties in children with ADHD. These deficits will be described in this chapter, as well as the behavioral and emotional difficulties that may contribute toward poor school performance in children with the disorder. The association of ADHD with dyslexia and the special problems of gifted children with ADHD are discussed at the end of the chapter.

Management of learning difficulties in children with ADHD is not dealt with in this chapter but is covered in Section 5.

Areas of difficulty

ADHD can affect any area of school performance, but language-based subjects are most commonly involved. Essay (story) writing is typically poor in children with ADHD. These children may have good ideas that they can express orally (oral expression) yet they find it extremely difficult to put their thoughts down on paper (written expression) in a coherent way. Their attempts usually consist of meagre amounts of poorly expressed written work. Spelling and reading comprehension are also often poor.

Some children with ADHD also have difficulties with oral expression and cannot give a coherent, sequential account of their experiences or ideas when speaking. They find it difficult to find the appropriate word when speaking ('word retrieval deficit') and may say the incorrect word as a result.

In a child with language-based learning difficulty, poor reading may impair the child's understanding of mathematical word problems. Nevertheless, for some children with ADHD, weakness in mathematics is unrelated to impairment in language-based learning. Such children experience mathematical difficulties that relate to deficits such as poor working memory and impulsivity that are described below.

For many children with ADHD, academic difficulty is not confined to a particular subject but occurs across a number of areas of study. In such children, weak organizational skills, lack of motivation, poor behavior in class, or an inability to get on with teachers or peers may be the cause of their poor grades. In some children with ADHD, the major problem is poor performance under examination conditions.

How problems become apparent

Children with severe processing or behavioral problems may encounter difficulties from their earliest school years. The teacher may observe that the child misunderstands instructions and is slow to start and to complete work. The child's work may be incomplete and he may not acquire basic skills such as reading or writing as rapidly as his peers.

Parents may note their child's extreme reluctance to do homework and his diminishing self-esteem in relation to schoolwork. He may make statements such as 'I am dumb!'. He may start feigning illness to avoid school. In some children with specific areas of difficulty, parents may notice that the child refuses to do specific parts of the homework (e.g. story writing) while enjoying others (e.g. maths). He may complain of being too ill to go to school on certain days when a particular subject is taught or tested.

Teachers may note that a child with the hyperactive form of ADHD is unable to remain seated and makes excuses to get out of his seat (e.g. to go to the toilet) if required to sit still for a protracted time. Some children with ADHD are talkative and disruptive in class; others gaze into space.

Children with the condition may manage the less demanding primary school years and only experience problems in high school. It is common for children with mild ADHD, particularly the inattentive type, to first encounter difficulties in high school.

Children with ADHD associated with behavioral problems may also experience greater difficulties in high school because at this time their behavior worsens due to the hormonal changes of puberty. The combination of ADHD, puberty, and the increasing demands of high school often cause problems to worsen, or to surface for the first time, in high school.

The causes of learning difficulty in ADHD

Poor concentration

Some children with ADHD absorb and retain very little information in the classroom because they are so easily distracted. They gaze out of the window, they stare into space, and their thoughts are far removed from the content of the lesson. Such a child may misunderstand the teacher's instructions and feel quite lost in the classroom. He may have to phone another child every afternoon to find out what homework has been set. He may be unaware of assignments that the teacher has set and deadlines that he must meet. His homework diary may be empty or filled with doodling and other scribbling unconnected with the lessons. In the class he may disturb others by talking. He will be slow to start work and, because he is so easily sidetracked, he will often fail to complete work in the allocated time. He may regularly have to stay in during breaks to complete work.

Such a child will find it very difficult to revise his work at home. He may remain in his room for long periods, ostensibly 'studying' but with very little actually achieved. He may find it impossible to stay in his room to study and so keep coming out, often with excuses that he needs a snack, to go for a walk, or some other diversion.

Such a child often finds it impossible to maintain the concentration required to read a book. School texts are not read or, if they are, the child's mind may wander so much that little of the content is retained. Poor concentration is the reason why reading comprehension is a particular weakness for children with ADHD.

While reading is difficult for such a child, there is no task more taxing for poor attentional mechanisms than writing. Writing provides very little immediate gratification: letters must be formed on the page one after another with no immediate reward. It is a very tedious process and children who are easily distracted often feel writing is a form of mental torture and they will go to great lengths to avoid it.

Some children with ADHD can concentrate reasonably well on their schoolwork, but lack attention to detail. This becomes a more significant problem as the child advances through school, work becomes more complex, and subtle distinctions and inferences become more important.

Impulsivity

The impulsivity of many children with ADHD can interfere with learning. Inability to reflect and to plan ahead leads to carelessness that can be a significant handicap in solving mathematical problems. In other subjects, too, the child's work may be compromised by a failure to stop and think. Impulsive children will answer a question without first giving it careful consideration.

Impulsivity impairs logical and sequential thinking and organization. (Poor working memory, another deficit that adversely affects these areas, is described below.) Children with impulsivity may also be 'slap-dash' in the way they carry out their work; they often have a 'near enough is good enough' approach to their homework and school assignments.

Working memory impairment

The poor working memory of children with ADHD is a very important cause of learning impairment.

As described in the first chapter, working memory is a temporary (short-term) store for information. By utilizing his working memory a child can understand the present in the light of his past knowledge; he can also keep in mind the steps of a plan while he implements it.

Poor working memory leads to difficulties in understanding texts, in carrying out multipart instructions, in planning written work, and in solving mathematical problems that require logical thinking.

A child with a poor working memory will struggle to understand the text he is reading because his mind cannot hold the part of the story he has already read while he continues reading. The parts of the story do not connect and no sooner has he finished a page, than it has been forgotten. He will therefore complain that the story makes no sense, or is 'boring'. He will find reading unrewarding and avoid it.

When given a series of instructions, a child with a poor working memory will not be able to hold them in his mind. He will forget the last steps of the task. Difficulties with sequencing may be related to poor working memory or, as described earlier in this chapter, to impulsivity.

Perhaps the greatest area of difficulty for children with poor working memory is in expressing themselves in speech (oral expression) or in writing (written expression). Their stories and speech are disorganized and incoherent. They often get lost in irrelevant detail and fail to see the wood for the trees.

Poor working memory is also implicated in reading (decoding) and spelling (encoding) difficulties in children with ADHD. Working memory plays a critical role in the early stages of learning to read and spell. This is when the brain is establishing a store of remembered words ('lexicon') that has to be accessed during the process of reading and spelling.

Defiance

Children with ADHD who are badly behaved in class will underachieve academically. This becomes a more significant problem in the last years of primary school or the early years of senior school when the hormonal changes of puberty compound the defiance associated with ADHD.

A defiant child will respond poorly to authority figures such as parents and teachers. Such a child will rebel against teachers who are overbearing, who teach subjects in which the child is weak, or who teach in a style that is not suited to the child (for example, a teacher who expects pupils to take down notes from dictation will not suit a child with poor auditory attention).

Adolescent boys with ADHD are often particularly averse to taking instruction from a woman teacher.

A child with ADHD will frequently develop an intense dislike for a particular teacher and then do little or no work for that teacher. By contrast, he may work very well for a teacher he admires. While it is true that most children without ADHD also work better for teachers they like than those they do not, it is the *total* lack of effort for a disliked teacher, and the refusal to modify this response, that is so characteristic of the child with ADHD.

Unfortunately, when a child misbehaves at school, his academic progress may be further impaired by attempts to discipline him. This occurs, for example, when he misses schoolwork because he is sent out of class, or suspended from attending school.

Low self-esteem

Low self-esteem is commonly present in children with ADHD and is a factor that may impede their academic progress.

Once a child's confidence in his ability is compromised, it becomes difficult for him to apply himself to his schoolwork. He will not make an effort to learn if he feels despondent about his chances of success. He will try to avoid embarrassing failures by strategies such as playing the 'class clown' (to cover up his academic difficulties), disrupting the class, refusing to go to school, truanting, and failing to hand in his work.

Because of the adverse effect on self-esteem, repeating a class usually has a negative impact on the educational progress of children with ADHD.

Low self-esteem also makes a child with ADHD respond particularly poorly if he feels that he has been humiliated in front of his peers by a teacher.

Social difficulties

Some teachers, particularly in the early school years, place great emphasis on group projects. Unfortunately, many children with ADHD work poorly in groups. They lack the 'give-and-take' necessary for group cooperation. They tend to be egocentric and overbearing with their peers. These characteristics, together with their inflexibility and low frustration tolerance, often lead to altercations in group work. If such work is an important component of the educational program, a child with ADHD may run into difficulties that interfere with his academic progress.

Poor incentival motivation

Progress in high school requires many hours of tedious study for a reward that may not be enjoyed until several years later. To succeed in high school, a child must be prepared to defer immediate gratification for later intangible rewards such as marks on his report card.

As described in the first chapter, this degree of forward planning and gratification deferment requires incentival motivation, an area of great difficulty for a child with ADHD. Children with the condition generally respond to their difficulties by blaming the work ('it is boring!') or by reducing their expectations and so underachieving academically.

These children tend to put off tasks to the last minute. Only when they are under a great deal of stress will they sometimes be able to work. This makes the problem difficult to distinguish from lack of willpower, but a comprehensive assessment (as described in Chapter 11) will uncover the nature of the child's difficulties.

Auditory processing impairment

Auditory processing deficits are common in children with ADHD. These deficits impair the ability of these children to make sense of what they hear. Their brains may not efficiently discriminate similar sounds from one another, retain words in the order they are spoken, or comprehend the meaning of language.

A child with auditory processing impairment will misunderstand instructions and so become confused by a teacher who teaches by talking a great deal. Often such a teacher will question whether the child has a hearing impairment because of his difficulties understanding the spoken word; however, hearing tests will be normal if the problem is ADHD. Special tests of auditory discrimination and processing, performed by a psychologist or speech therapist, will uncover the true nature of the child's difficulties.

Spelling difficulties

Children with ADHD often experience difficulties with spelling. There are basically three types of spelling error seen in the work of these children:

Visual errors   These errors sound correct, but look wrong. Examples are 'lite' for 'light' and 'grate' for 'great'. These mistakes are due to poor visual memory and lack of attention to detail. They are the most common type of error seen in the work of children with ADHD.

Sequential errors   These cause mistakes such as 'brigde' for 'bridge'. They are due to sequencing problems associated with poor working memory, poor concentration, and impulsivity.

Phonetic errors   These are the least common difficulty in these children. Such errors will have some visual resemblance to the correct spelling, but sound different when read. For example, the child may write 'lap' for 'lip' or 'goase' for 'goose'. These errors are more common if the child has co-existing dyslexia (see below).

Handwriting difficulties

Children with ADHD are often poorly coordinated and are clumsy when manipulating objects (poor fine-motor skills). Handwriting is often slow and untidy in children with the disorder.

If a child is able to perform any of the actions involved in forming letters in isolation, but cannot carry out these actions in an uninterrupted sequence when writing, the difficulty is known as 'motor dyspraxia'. The handwriting of a child with motor dyspraxia is slow and untidy.

Organizational difficulties

Organizational skills are very poor in most children with ADHD. This will have a negative impact on their schoolwork, particularly in their high school years when teachers expect and demand a great deal of self-sufficiency from their pupils.

Even bright children with ADHD will obtain poor marks if they forget to bring work and books home, fail to plan ahead for projects and study, and fail to hand in their work for marking.

Dyslexia and ADHD

Dyslexia is a specific difficulty in learning that interferes with a child's ability to learn to read. It occurs because of an abnormality in brain function that is usually inherited. Although dyslexia can be an isolated problem in a child, *it is much more common in children with ADHD than children who do not have ADHD* (see the section on 'co-morbidity' in Chapter 1).

When a well-behaved child with dyslexia has the inattentive form of ADHD, his learning difficulties may be incorrectly ascribed to the dyslexia alone. This occurs because many parents, and even some professionals, regard ADHD exclusively as a behavioral problem. They make the mistake of thinking that a child's good behavior excludes ADHD.

If a child who has dyslexia and ADHD receives remedial teaching alone he will usually make little or no progress because impairments in working memory and attention to detail will continue to block learning. With time the child's self-esteem diminishes and it becomes even less likely that he will overcome his difficulties. In such a child, it is often only when medication to treat the ADHD is *combined* with the remedial program that real progress is made and maintained.

Such children usually need a very small dose of medication to cover school days only. A dramatic improvement in the child's self-esteem and academic progress is often noticed in a matter of days after commencing treatment.

The gifted child with ADHD

Since ADHD is unrelated to intelligence, the proportion of gifted individuals is no different among those with ADHD than those without. The presence of ADHD, however, presents three special problems to a gifted child.

First, the performance of gifted children is sensitive to even very mild degrees of ADHD. It seems that small impairments in working memory and organizational skills have a disproportionately severe impact on the performance of a gifted child.

Such children may not score below average in their areas of difficulty, they may only score significantly less well than they do in other areas. It is therefore important that treatment of ADHD be considered in any gifted child who is experiencing academic difficulties, even if tests show very mild degrees of the impairment.

Second, in a gifted child who has ADHD, both the giftedness and the ADHD may be missed. This occurs when the learning impairment associated with the ADHD reduces the child's academic performance from above average (where it should be) to an average level. Parents and teachers may be satisfied that the child seems to be performing in the average range of performance without realizing the child's true potential. Only an astute parent or teacher will suspect that the child is underachieving. A comprehensive assessment, as described in Chapter 11, will uncover the true nature of both the child's gifts and his disability.

Third, in some gifted children with ADHD who are underachieving, the child's exceptional gifts may be detected, but the presence of co-existing ADHD missed. This occurs when the child's underachievement is wrongly ascribed to boredom or lack of motivation. Such explanations should never be accepted without a proper assessment to exclude other causes of the child's underperformance.

6
Defiance

Approximately one quarter of children with ADHD experience significant difficulties conforming to the rules and regulations appropriate for their age. These difficulties are usually seen both at home and at school, although some children can cope with a very structured situation at school and experience all their difficulties in the home setting.

This defiant behavior is often misunderstood by observers who think that there must be something wrong with the way that the parents are disciplining their child.

Parents of such children often report that their friends, as well as strangers, will make suggestions, such as 'you are not being tough enough', or 'if you gave him a good hiding he would stop doing that'. Unfortunately the management of defiant behavior in children with ADHD is not so simple.

Compliance—a function of the brain

Normal toddlers have great difficulty complying with their parents' instructions. The phrase 'terrible twos' is widely used to describe the great difficulty that children have between the ages of about 15 months and 3 years in obeying parental commands. At that stage of development, the brain is simply not mature enough to allow the child to inhibit self-centered needs, to delay gratification, and to conform. At that stage the brain has not yet developed its mechanism that we generally call 'conscience'. Children of that age are not yet able to put themselves into someone else's place and to understand how their behavior is affecting others. They simply act out their feelings and do the things they feel they want to do, without regard to the consequences.

As the brain develops, this lawlessness is inhibited by the increasing activity of the frontal lobe. It has been known for a long time that adults who sustain damage to certain parts of the brain can start behaving in a defiant, non-compliant manner (just like 'terrible twos').

In many children with ADHD, the necessary mechanisms for compliance with rules and regulations develop slowly. This means that although the child is in an ordinary home and ordinary school, he cannot conform like other children of his age.

Our society has great difficulty accepting this. We feel uncomfortable with the idea that children who are behaving poorly may be doing so because of a brain disorder. We like to have someone to blame for the child's difficulties and we focus on the child's parents.

In fact, children with ADHD with non-compliant behavior have parents who are just as competent as other parents. They are usually at their wit's end to know what to do with their extremely difficult child. Many have experience of raising children without behavior problems, and are at a loss to know how to deal with a child who does not respond to the usual methods of discipline.

Parents of such children quickly learn that smacking and other forms of punishment are ineffective. They are therefore forced into passive acceptance of much unwanted behavior, which only seems to confirm the casual observer's view that they are being too lenient. Such observers often do not realize that the parents have been forced to become lenient because other strategies have failed. If they were to smack their child, or use 'time out', whenever he perpetrated a misdemeanor, they would be forced to smack the child continually, or he would have to spend most of his waking hours locked in his room.

Another aspect of such children's behavior is its variability. This also leads to misunderstanding. For example, an 8 year old with ADHD who has the compliance of a 2 year old will be very inconsistent in the way in which he behaves in different situations. This is why parents often use the term 'Jekyll and Hyde' to describe their child. It is not simply that the child is never compliant. At certain times, for example when he is not tired or when he tries extremely hard, he will be successful in behaving well. However, he cannot maintain this for protracted periods of time, or in all the situations that a child of his age should be able to. Sometimes he will be better with one parent, usually the father. This may be because he is less familiar with his father, or because the father is quicker to resort to painful physical discipline.

Unfortunately, such performance inconsistency, which is a prominent feature of ADHD, is often misinterpreted as implying that the child could succeed if only he tried. This is analogous to saying that because a child with heart disease can walk 15 m without becoming breathless, he should be able to run a marathon, if only he tried hard enough. It is the difficulty with *sustained* performance that shows up the problems of the child with ADHD, in the same way as it does for the child with heart disease. Sustained performance is the true test of the competence and maturity of the brain functions that are impaired in children with ADHD.

Observers may think that children with ADHD should be able to comply with rules because they know and understand them. But ADHD is a *performance* disability, not a *knowledge* disability. Children with ADHD usually know what they should do and should not do; they simply cannot consistently do the things that they know they should.

Severity of defiant behavior

Non-compliant behavior in children with ADHD can be divided into two forms. The more common, milder form, is known as *oppositional disorder*, while the more severe, fortunately more rare, form is known as *conduct disorder*.

Oppositional disorder

Approximately one quarter of all children with ADHD have oppositional behavior. Such children demonstrate several of the following behaviors:

Active defiance

Children with oppositional disorder will flout rules. They often refuse to do their homework, to carry out household chores, or to conform to requests such as wearing a complete school uniform. Any child without ADHD may defy adult instructions, but children with oppositional behavior do this in a far more extreme way, persisting despite repeated punishment.

Argumentativeness

Parents will often say that, with the child who has oppositional behavior, 'every discussion is an argument'. Often the only communication between parent and child is in the form of arguments. Children with oppositional behavior will characteristically argue with all adults, including teachers and even strangers, in a way that other children of the same age would not do.

Temper outbursts

Children with oppositional disorder have temper tantrums of the kind that are usually not seen in school-age children. They resemble the tantrums seen in toddlers.

Often parents will report that their child will be reasonable until any of his desires are thwarted or frustrated in any way. He will then suddenly have a temper tantrum, kicking walls, slamming doors, and shouting. If put in his room for 'time out' (see Chapter 14) he may totally destroy his possessions. Some will even escape through the window.

The temper tantrums may be so sudden, and so out of proportion to what has happened, that parents may think the child is having some form of seizure. An unusual form of epilepsy (temporal lobe epilepsy) does have to be considered in any child who has unprovoked temper outbursts; however, in children with oppositional disorder it is not that the temper tantrum is unprovoked, it is simply that the trigger is so insignificant.

Deliberately annoying and provoking other individuals

Children with oppositional disorder tend to interfere with others. They seem to be unable to resist the temptation to provoke other children. Often they cannot go past a sibling without punching him or her. In the playground, teachers may notice that the child with oppositional disorder will grab another child's possessions and run off with them so as to provoke him or her. Such children often have no understanding of their own vulnerability and will provoke children who are much larger than themselves without realizing the consequences.

'Touchiness'

Children with oppositional behavior are extremely easily annoyed. They will be slighted by the most minor action and then will become very angry and aggressive. Once more, it is the frequency and severity of these outbursts that distinguish them from similar behavior in a normal child.

Projection of blame

Children with oppositional behavior tend to blame others for their own inadequacies. Any mistake on their part is immediately attributed to someone else such as a parent, a teacher, or a friend.

Resentfulness

Children with oppositional disorder often deeply resent any authority figure. They will therefore complain bitterly about anyone who tries to discipline them. They may be quick to develop a deep hatred for any authority figures they come across.

Spitefulness and vindictiveness

These are characteristics often seen in children with oppositional behavior. For no apparent reason, they will try to hurt another person. It is usually siblings who suffer the most from this sort of behavior, but sometimes parents will notice that a child with oppositional behavior will behave spitefully toward a younger child on first meeting. They may be very cruel to children who are weak or vulnerable in some way.

They tend to bear grudges and will seek revenge long after any real or imagined misdemeanor against them.

Swearing

Even from an early age, children with oppositional behavior are quick to learn swear words. They will often use obscene language in a situation where a child of their age would know that this is not appropriate. The best way to handle swearing is to ignore it, but this often does not resolve the problem in these children.

Conduct disorder

Conduct disorder is more severe than oppositional disorder and occurs in about 7% of children with ADHD. Conduct disorder differs from oppositional disorder in that the problems attract a greater degree of social disapproval, and often result in the child breaking the law.

Some children will develop conduct disorder at an early age, even as early as 7 or 8 years. Most, however, start off with oppositional disorder and then develop conduct disorder in the teenage years. Most are male.

Some children with conduct disorder are the 'solitary aggressive' type. These children are loners and carry out their offences on their own. More common are the 'group type offenders', who are attracted to other children with similar problems. Group type offenders may behave quite reasonably when on their own, but become anti-social when part of their group (gang).

The behaviors seen in children with conduct disorder include the following:

Stealing

Children with conduct disorder steal often and repeatedly. They may do this *without confrontation*, where possessions are taken when the owner is absent, or *with confrontation*, when they threaten the owner before removing the possession. Stealing with confrontation is of even greater concern than stealing without confrontation, because it may be accompanied by assault.

Running away

It is rare for children with conduct disorder not to have run away from home overnight on at least two occasions. Often this becomes a repeated pattern of behavior and parents may not know where their child is for long stretches of time.

Repeated lying

Normal children may lie in order to avoid punishment or to impress their friends. Children with oppositional behavior also lie in order to obtain something that they want. In fact, lying becomes so common that it becomes very difficult for parents to know when the child is telling the truth and when he is not.

Setting fires

Normal or oppositional children may play with matches on occasions. Some children with conduct disorder are more persistent in the way in which they set fires. Rather than simply experimenting with matches, they will try to burn down buildings such as their school or home.

Truanting

Children with conduct disorder will spend a great deal of time wagging school (see School avoidance, Chapter 7).

Breaking-in

Breaking-in to a house, a building, or a car is common in children with conduct disorder. This may be associated with stealing or joyriding, or may be an end in itself.

Destroying property

Children with oppositional disorder often have a compulsion to damage things. They may destroy their toys and other possessions.

Children with conduct disorder will often go about destroying other people's possessions. They may walk through the streets breaking windows and damaging cars. They often resent other people having possessions that they do not have.

Spray-painting walls is becoming an increasingly common behavior among children with conduct disorder. Painting graffiti can become an obsessional behavior for some children with conduct disorder.

Cruelty to animals

Children with conduct disorder often lack the compassion toward animals that is usually seen in children. They seem to enjoy taking advantage of animals' vulnerability, and parents will sometimes become aware that their child is becoming cruel in the way in which he treats pets and other neighborhood animals. On occasion, children with conduct disorder have behaved cruelly toward animals in zoos and wildlife parks.

Forcing sexual activity

Forcing sexual activity is more common in the 'group type' of child with conduct disorder. The perpetrators are usually male and the victims are usually female.

Using weapons

Many children with conduct disorder are fascinated by weapons. They may start collecting knives and even firearms. Some will try to use these.

Initiating fights

Children with conduct disorder seem to enjoy getting into fights. They may regularly come home having been involved in some altercation. These may be with other groups or with individuals.

The characteristic of children with conduct disorder is that they initiate fights and seek out confrontation.

Physical cruelty to people

Younger siblings are often the first victims of this form of violence. While it is quite normal for siblings to argue and fight, the behavior of children with conduct disorder is characterized by the degree of cruelty shown toward younger siblings.

A younger sibling is in a very vulnerable situation. The younger child cannot physically defend him or herself from the older, stronger individual with whom he or she must share the home. Often the older sibling will wait until the parents' backs are turned and then do all he can to batter the sibling.

Little attention has been directed toward 'sibling abuse', or 'domestic violence against siblings'. Some siblings are assaulted in a way that would result in legal proceedings if this had not occurred within the home. Parents have a responsibility toward the younger sibling to ensure that he or she is not subjected to such treatment.

Treatment of defiant behavior

Oppositional disorder

Mild oppositional behavior will often resolve with medication alone. Once a child is on appropriate medication for ADHD, he usually becomes calmer and his behavior more compliant. Aggression also decreases.

It is helpful if parents also learn behavior management techniques so that they can implement these together with the medical treatment (see Chapter 14).

For children with more severe oppositional disorder, behavior management needs to be looked at in greater detail. In such cases, it is important that a psychologist is involved to provide parents with appropriate strategies for managing their child's behavior. These, used in conjunction with medication, will not totally eradicate the behaviors, but will ensure that the child is more manageable and is less likely to do harm to himself or others. It also makes the later development of conduct disorder less likely.

Conduct disorder

Management of conduct disorder is extremely difficult. There are some children with conduct disorder who will respond positively to medication, so medication should always be tried. Unfortunately, medication does not help many children with conduct disorder. Even in those children where medication is helpful, it can be extremely difficult to get the child to take it consistently. Such children often deny that the medication helps them, even when it is quite clear to parents and other observers that it does! Parents may need to exert a lot of energy in order to ensure that medicine is taken.

Children with conduct disorder often experiment with alcohol and marijuana and parents often wonder whether medicines used for ADHD will interact with these. Medicines that are used in ADHD do not interact in any specific adverse way with alcohol or marijuana. However, marijuana and alcohol tend to make children poorly motivated and lacking in inhibition, while the medicines used for ADHD make them better focused and motivated. Marijuana and alcohol therefore undermine the effect of the medicine the child is taking.

It is important that parents of a child with conduct disorder receive counseling to help them develop strategies for coping with their child's behavior. Most parents will need someone outside the family to talk to them about their concerns, and to look at different ways of dealing with their child's behavior.

Parents of a child with conduct disorder are in an extremely difficult situation. They want to keep the child out of trouble, but the child often seems bent on a course of self-destruction. All that parents can do is to try to be available when their child needs them, and hope that with time the brain will mature and the behavior settle.

There certainly are no easy answers to questions about the appropriateness of special school units or special residential units for children with conduct disorder. These issues need to be looked at on an individual basis. The decision about whether to involve the police can also be a difficult one when the child's aggression is directed toward parents or their property. If the child's behavior is placing others at risk, the police may have to be involved.

Individual psychotherapy (counseling) can have a role in some children, but this, like other forms of treatment, is often ineffective. Children with conduct disorder tend to sabotage most forms of treatment.

While some children with conduct disorder will end up in prison, others do undergo a miraculous maturation in their late teens or early twenties and do not get into any further trouble. Many an adult who is now a good citizen had a very stormy childhood.

7
Low self-esteem

It is hard to think of any attribute more crucial to success in life than high self-esteem. Whatever abilities a child may have, without a good self-image she is unlikely to succeed. If success does come to an individual with a low self-esteem, it is unlikely to be enjoyed.

Most children with ADHD suffer from a low self-esteem. This may become apparent to the parents when the child makes negative comments such as 'I am dumb!' or 'I can't do this!' In some children, poor self-esteem may show itself by excessive moodiness, irritability, tearfulness, or withdrawal. In other children, problems with self-esteem may not be apparent. Difficult behaviors such as aggression, an excessive desire to control situations, distaste for being cuddled, and excessive quitting can all be attempts to maintain a fragile self-esteem. It is easy to misinterpret such behavior as defiant or perverse. Unfortunately, if the origin of these behaviors is not recognized, attempts to correct them may further undermine the child's self-esteem.

Self-appraisal—a function of the brain

We all know individuals who have been successful, but who have poor feelings of self-worth; and there are many people who have not been successful, or who have not had good experiences during their lives, who maintain a positive estimation of their own value.

It seems that there are important mechanisms in the brain that control the way in which children evaluate themselves and cope with things that go wrong in their day-to-day experience. Stella Chess and Alexander Thomas were the first to describe the noticeable differences in temperament that babies demonstrate almost immediately after birth. Studies of alteration of self-appraisal in adults who have undergone brain injuries, as well as after the effects of drugs that act on the brain, give further support to a biological, brain-based component to self-esteem.

The part of the brain that controls self-esteem is widely believed to be the limbic system that lies deep within the frontal part of the brain. The frontal parts of the brain receive highly processed and filtered sensory information from other parts of the brain. That information eventually reaches the limbic system that regulates emotional responses and feelings. As explained in Chapter 10, the frontal lobes of the brain do not function normally in children with ADHD.

This would explain why many of the characteristics of self-appraisal in children with ADHD are immature. For example, very young children tend to look for someone or something to blame for things that go wrong. A young child who hurts herself may become angry and aggressive, looking for someone to blame for the accident. She therefore projects the 'locus of blame' onto her mother or siblings (or even an inanimate object). As children develop they become less likely to look for a locus of blame for things that go wrong. They can accept the fact that accidents occur, and shrug off difficulties with a reasonable amount of equanimity.

A child with ADHD will often retain this tendency to look for a locus of blame beyond the age where it usually disappears. Misfortune may give rise to anger and aggression directed toward others who were not responsible for what happened.

Children with ADHD will often project the locus of blame onto themselves and therefore appraise themselves harshly for things that go wrong. Conversely, if things go well they may not attribute this to their own ability. It becomes clear that they have not developed an appropriate feeling of autonomy or competence that is necessary for adequate feelings of self-worth. This can be seen in the way in which they respond to their achievements. A normal child who passes an examination will be able to feel good about his or her achievements. A child with ADHD may say something like 'the questions were very easy', or 'the teacher gave me more marks because she knows I am dumb!'.

With an immature appraisal system, children with ADHD can easily come to attribute negative intentions to other people when these intentions do not exist. They are therefore quick to feel threatened and discouraged. It is characteristic of many children with ADHD that they always expect the worst and that they have difficulties in seeing good in others or themselves.

It is easy to see how children with ADHD can become depressed. Depression is a form of anger directed at oneself, and children who project blame onto themselves, and feel that they are not capable or competent, can easily become sad and withdrawn.

Children with ADHD are thus doubly at risk of experiencing problems with self-esteem. First, they have many difficulties in their everyday performance due to their problems with poor attention span, impulsivity, poor social cognition, and difficulties with learning. They, therefore, often experience failure and criticism. Second, they have problems with self-appraisal that lead them to quickly lose feelings of self-worth.

Control of the self-appraisal system in the brain

We still know little about how the self-appraisal system that controls self-esteem works. However, it seems certain that levels of neurotransmitters play an important role.

Neurotransmitters are chemicals produced at the end of nerves in the brain to send a message from one nerve cell to another. As will be discussed in the Chapter 10, low levels of certain neurotransmitters are the basic cause of ADHD.

Although many people have difficulty understanding how chemicals in the brain can control self-esteem, most people have personal experience of temporarily 'adjusting' their self-appraisal mechanisms by changing the levels of neurotransmitter in the brain. They do this by drinking alcohol. Many people will have had the experience of feeling more capable after an alcoholic drink. For example, public speakers will sometimes have a drink of alcohol to 'steady their nerves' before speaking.

Alcohol works by altering neurotransmitter levels. (This is the way most drugs affect the brain.) The individual experiences an improved feeling of self-worth and confidence while the alcohol is active. Alcohol often makes the speech worse, but nevertheless, the speaker thinks he is doing much better. This is a clear demonstration that self-esteem and actual performance are not necessarily connected.

Drinking alcohol to 'steady the nerves' is to be avoided. However, it does demonstrate that self-esteem is at least partially controlled by neurotransmitters. The speaker who has fortified himself with alcohol becomes less competent and yet feels far more competent. Of course, once the alcohol wears off, confidence decreases and there might even be a rebound effect, whereby the individual feels that he has performed poorly.

Dysfunctional coping behaviors

Many unwanted behaviors that are seen in children with ADHD are due to problems with self-esteem. It is essential that parents and teachers recognize this before trying to treat the behavior. Often such behaviors cannot be eradicated without helping the child gain better feelings of self-worth, something that may take time.

It is very easy to become frustrated with these behaviors and criticize the child. However, this will only lower the child's feeling of self-worth further and entrench the behavior, or force the child to substitute other unwanted behaviors.

All of these behaviors are attempts on the part of the child to deflect feelings of inadequacy and to prevent them from getting worse. In most cases the attempts are only partially successful, and treatment should aim to find successful ways of reducing the negative feelings.

Here are some examples of dysfunctional behaviors, together with some advice about managing them.

Quitting

Some children develop a habit of quitting as a way of coping with feelings of inadequacy. When frustrated, because they cannot win a game or accomplish a skill, they will quit. They often will offer an excuse, such as that the task or game was 'stupid' or 'boring'. In both school-work and in games, they give up the moment they encounter difficulties and then refuse to continue.

It is no use entering into a discussion with the child about the importance of the activity, or insisting that it is not boring. The child's criticism of the activity is simply a smokescreen that she raises in order to protect herself from failure. Arguing about this is not going to resolve the issue. In fact, by arguing that the activity is important, you only increase her anxiety about failing.

It is important that you make certain that the tasks your child attempts are within her capabilities. If a task or game is difficult, try to find a substitute that is within her capabilities. Try to give her special jobs to do that require a small degree of persistence, and have a reward system for when she finishes these. In this way she will have the opportunity to learn that persistence does pay. Tell her stories about great people who did not give up when they were facing defeat. Children's libraries usually have books that teach children particular virtues, like courage or persistence.

Most importantly, try to take the tension out of the situation. Make activities as much fun as possible. Join in where possible and show that you too make mistakes, but that you do not become upset.

Avoiding

Avoiding is similar to quitting, except the individual does not even start the activity. Children with ADHD will often not want to join in activities, or to volunteer to take part, for fear of failing. Children with ADHD often refuse to make arrangements to visit a friend, do not want to try for a part in a play, or will not put their hand up in class because of problems with poor self-esteem. Their feeling of self-worth is so low that they feel that they cannot afford to fail.

It is essential that such children should not be criticized. They need to be directed toward activities in which they can succeed and where they are not in the limelight.

Adverse responses to praise

Children with low self-esteem might behave in an adverse way when praised. Instead of enjoying praise, they may become angry or negative whenever praise is given. Because they feel so inadequate, any praise is misinterpreted and regarded as implied criticism. Praise often reminds them of how far they fall below their own expectations and what they believe to be the expectations of the person who is praising them. They interpret the praise as being patronizing and containing implied criticism.

In such a situation, praise should be used sparingly and only when it is clear that the child feels satisfied with her performance. Praise the child's accomplishment rather than the child herself. Wherever possible, encourage the child to praise herself, but do not persevere if it is clear that she does not feel comfortable about doing this.

Tactile defensiveness

Children with ADHD often do not like being touched or cuddled. This aversion to touch is known as 'tactile defensiveness'. Parents often become hurt at this, believing that the child does not feel affectionate toward them. The truth is that children with ADHD often do not feel happy about being cuddled because of their low self-esteem. Often if a child does not feel good about herself, she will not enjoy being touched. This is because being cuddled makes her feel very vulnerable to rejection and because, strange as it may seem to the parent, the child does not feel loved or lovable.

Parents have to be patient with children who have tactile defensiveness. They have to strike a happy balance between not forcing themselves upon the child, and at the same time trying to make some physical contact that they hope will increase as the child becomes more confident. Knowing exactly what to do does require an ability to 'read' the child's feelings.

Parents naturally want to cuddle and comfort an upset child. However, children with ADHD who have low self-esteem may be best left alone when they are upset, and may feel happiest sitting on their own or retreating to their room. The time to touch the child may be when the child is feeling happier and more confident. Touch should be very limited initially, increasing gradually as the child is desensitized. Many children with ADHD benefit from having soft toys that they can cuddle without fear of rejection.

Cheating

Some children learn to cope with failure by cheating. This may occur at school, when work is copied, or at home. The child feels so certain that she cannot win a game or pass a test that she alters rules and copies answers.

You should make certain that your child is not being set tasks that are beyond her capabilities. You should also make certain that she is not receiving criticism for her failure. The child should be praised for her effort, even if her work is incorrect.

If teachers spot that a child is cheating, they should only mark the portion of the work that they feel the child has done herself and ignore the rest. In this way she learns that she is rewarded only for her own efforts.

It is best if you do not let your child get away with significant lying or cheating. Whenever she is caught at it, ask her if she understands what she is doing. Explain that you admire her efforts whether she succeeds or fails, but that cheating spoils games and work. Talk to her about this, mentioning that you understand why she wants to cheat, but explain how much better it is to be honest. Ensure that honesty is praised. In games, set an example of how to lose gracefully.

Lying

There are two forms of lying seen in children with ADHD. Some children will lie in order to get what they want (offensive lying). This is to be discouraged and it is important for parents to ensure that children do not gain advantage by telling untruths.

A more common form of lying seen in children with ADHD is when children lie to get out of trouble (defensive lying). This is a form of coping with low self-esteem. It is important not to put your child into a situation where she has to lie frequently. Parents should not ask their child if she is guilty when they suspect that she might have carried out some misdemeanor. By continually being put 'on the spot' in this way, the child is forced to lie in order to 'save face'. It is better if you only criticize your child when you know she has done something wrong. In such a situation it is unnecessary for you to ask whether or not she was guilty.

In those situations where you do not know if she has done something wrong, it would be better not to ask her difficult questions, whenever possible. Defensive lying often quickly resolves when parents cut down on the amount of cross-examining that they do.

Clowning

Children with low self-esteem will often play the part of the clown in order to gain attention and feel good about themselves. They will also feel that they can avoid activities in which they may fail by playing the part of the incompetent. Often children will inadvertently say something funny in class and then, when they realize the approbation that this brings, will continue to play this part. Other children are often only too willing to let the child with ADHD make a fool of herself in this way. Unfortunately, clowning rarely wins true friends for the child and makes her susceptible to ridicule. She may then find it difficult for other children to take her seriously when she wants them to.

Clowning is usually seen in the classroom and it is important that teachers tackle this appropriately. Punishing the child who plays the part of the clown only decreases her self-worth and encourages further subversive clowning. Rather, the teacher should try to stop the other children from laughing at the child and thereby reinforcing her behavior.

Regressive behavior

Children often behave in an immature fashion as a way of coping with stress. Children with ADHD who have self-esteem problems may behave in a babyish way because they are frightened of failing. By adopting a childish manner, they subconsciously hope to convey the impression that they are too young to be criticized for their failure. They tend to persist with this behavior if it is successful.

A certain amount of regressive behavior can be accepted, but if it is clear that the child is behaving in a babyish way too often, parents should make certain that mature behavior is praised and regressive behavior ignored and discouraged.

School avoidance

Children with ADHD may avoid going to school. This may take a number of forms. The child may flatly refuse to leave home, she may frequently complain that she is ill, she may pretend that she is going off to school but never arrive, or she may leave school during the course of the day by absconding or saying she is ill.

Those who complain of being ill may be feigning illness, or they may be so anxious about going to school that they actually experience stress-related symptoms, such as abdominal pain and headaches.

This sort of school avoidance is usually due to distress about academic or social difficulties. She may be frightened of failing, or being teased or ostracized. Sometimes a child tries to avoid particular lessons, for example mathematics in the case of a child with particular difficulties with arithmetic, or physical education in a clumsy child. Parents may see a pattern in the days the child misses.

A distinction should be drawn between this sort of school avoidance and the intense fear of school (school phobia) that is often associated with issues related to leaving home, rather than anxiety about school itself.

If your child is avoiding school, speak to her about it. You should also speak to her teacher to see if there are academic or social stresses that can be reduced.

It is important to prevent school avoidance becoming a regular pattern of behavior. If you feel that your child is feigning illness, do not give her excessive attention. Give her bland food when she is at home and do not let her spend time watching the TV. Be matter of fact and encourage attendance at school, even if only for half the day. It is important to keep in touch with the school and have work sent home which she is expected to do. There should be a clear expectation that she will return to school at the earliest possible opportunity.

If these simple measures do not work, it is best to involve your child's doctor or a psychologist. This is particularly important if your child is refusing to leave her room or if she is very withdrawn.

Homework avoidance

Homework avoidance often leads to a great deal of conflict between parents and children with ADHD. If your child is not completing her homework, you should first check whether it is too difficult, or too much, for her. If so, speak to her teacher about this.

If the level and amount of homework is appropriate, but your child is still having difficulties, you may need to look at how she goes about the work. Do not be tempted to do the work for her, but help her learn to organize herself efficiently. You will need to look at when she does the homework, where she does it, and how she arranges the time to do it.

It is usually best if there is a specified homework time. For some children with ADHD, this may need to follow a chance to burn off energy in active play. For other children, it may be better to leave the play as a reward for after the homework is completed. Whichever time is chosen, there should be some specified reward for when the work is completed. The child needs as quiet an environment as possible. Many children work best if there is a parent nearby, even though he or she may not need to take an active part in helping the child. For such children, the parent's presence has a settling effect. Homework should not go on for too long. If there is a lot of work to cover, or if your child is slow, it may need to be broken up into a couple of sessions.

It is important that you teach your child how to manage her time effectively. She needs to know how to arrange work according to priorities, and how to work systematically. Teach her not to expect you to do all the work for her, but to think of you as a resource that she can call upon when she needs advice.

Children may need particular help if a project needs to be completed over a long period. Help your child to break this into stages and to create a timetable for completing each stage. Without this help, things will often be left to the last minute and the child then feels overwhelmed.

TV 'addiction'

Parents of children with ADHD often complain that their child spends a lot of time watching TV. Difficulties with academic work, as well as with social relationships, mean that TV is a common diversion for this group of children.

Limiting the amount of TV is only part of the answer. It is important to find rewarding substitute activities. You may be able to find after-school activities for your child, based on her interests. Keep an eye on local newspapers and talk to other parents to find out about suitable activities for children. You may also obtain information from local sports and recreation centers. If your child is having difficulties making friends, she may benefit from attending a social skills group. You need to check with your local health center whether one is being run in your area.

Aggression

Aggressive behavior is a common cover for low self-esteem. A child who feels that she has failed may vent her anger on others. A child who does not feel good about herself may derive satisfaction by exerting power over others. Such a child may get into fights, bully other children, or engage in arguments and make critical remarks about siblings and others.

Listen carefully to what your child says when she insults others; she is probably echoing the criticisms that hurt her most. If this is the case, you need to check on why she feels that she is being criticized in this way, and take steps to stop it. Check whether she is being victimized at school; she may be part of a pecking order and simply acting out the aggression she is experiencing.

Determine whether she is behaving aggressively only in certain situations and see if you can identify what provokes the behavior. Often outbursts occur at times when your child experiences a failure, or threat of failure. It may be possible to avoid such situations, or to change things so that your child does not feel inadequate.

For some children, it may be necessary to arrange a reward system for not losing their temper. You should also teach your child strategies for coping with her aggressive feelings. She may go for a walk, jump on a trampoline, or listen to music. Sometimes a child will benefit from a punch bag, or even a pillow on which she can vent her anger. Encourage her to express to you the way she feels and accept these feelings with sympathy.

If aggressive outbursts remain a problem despite these measures, it is a good idea to seek help from your child's doctor or psychologist. If the habit of resorting to aggressive outbursts becomes ingrained, it may be difficult to eradicate later and may cause much trouble in adulthood.

Controlling behavior

Many children with low self-esteem feel that they have so little control over their own lives that they feel quite helpless. Some children respond by trying to command and dominate others. They tell people what to do, defy adults, and generally seek to dominate and control situations.

The best way to manage such behavior is to give the child some areas where she does have control, for example choosing her clothes, helping to select items at the supermarket, and deciding how to spend her pocket money (within reason!). Allocate some pleasant task that becomes her responsibility and reward her for doing it. Explain that certain tasks are her domain but others are not.

When giving instructions, do this in the form of choices whenever possible: 'Do you want to tidy up your room while I do the lounge?', or 'Will you do the lounge while I do your room?'. This is less likely to make her feel that she is losing autonomy.

Passive aggression

Some children with ADHD develop behavior that is passively aggressive. There is no overt aggression, but the child subverts attempts to control her. For example, she will promise to meet certain responsibilities, but then 'forgets' to do so. She may sabotage attempts by parents to achieve goals by failing to turn up to planned activities when required. Such children avoid confrontation, but make it extremely difficult for parents to control them.

Management of passive aggressive behavior combines techniques described in the two previous sections under the headings 'Aggression' and 'Controlling behavior'. Children with passive aggressive behavior should be given more control over their lives and allowed to express their anger verbally. Sometimes such children need individual counseling so that they can express their suppressed feelings of anger.

Denial

Another behavior that is commonly seen in children with low self-esteem is a tendency to deny difficulties. In this way they can deal with the feelings of hurt that may result if they were to acknowledge their limitations and vulnerability. When asked about their concerns they will simply state that they do not care about things, or that things are going well. Once more, counseling may be needed to help such children talk about their difficulties.

Rationalization

As children with ADHD get older they may start offering many excuses for their difficulties and failures. For example, a child caught cheating might argue that she was disadvantaged in some way in the examination and that, therefore, it was appropriate that she compensate for this by looking at someone else's work. After failing a test she may start criticizing specific shortcomings in the test as a way of maintaining her self-esteem.

With children who tend to rationalize, it is important not to become involved in arguments that attack their defences. Rather, it is important to recognize the origin of the child's rationalization—the need to maintain self-esteem—and to find ways of bolstering the child's feelings. Sometimes all that is necessary is to listen to the child and acknowledge the feelings of frustration that she is experiencing.

Impulsivity

Impulsivity is a primary characteristic of ADHD, but might also be seen as a response to difficulties with self-esteem. Children may cope with their difficulties by sudden impulsive acts in an attempt to 'just get it over with'. They are satisfied with a 'near enough is good enough' approach to their work and everything they do is 'slapdash'.

The importance of self-esteem maintenance mechanisms

The behaviors discussed above are strategies that all children use at some time to maintain their self-esteem. Children with ADHD are different in that they are more likely to use these mechanisms in a counter-productive way. They are not thought out by the children, but are strategies they come across by accident and then recruit as part of their protective shield. In all cases they are attempts by the child to maintain his or her feeling of self-worth.

The primary aim of any treatment should be to maintain the child's feeling of self-esteem. One can, therefore, not simply remove these defence mechanisms without putting something else in their place.

8
Social clumsiness

Children with ADHD may experience social difficulties because of features of their condition, such as over-activity, impulsivity, and low self-esteem. In addition, many children with ADHD have a limitation in the way in which their brain is able to understand and respond to social conventions. This is called a social cognition deficit.

Social cognition—a function of the brain

Much of what children learn about socially appropriate behavior is not actually taught to them; they simply pick it up as they go along. For them to do this, certain parts of the brain need to develop to an appropriate maturity for the child's age. The child with ADHD seems to have an immaturity in the part of the brain responsible for social cognition and so is less able to learn socially appropriate behavior, even when taught.

Such a child experiences difficulty in behaving in a way that is socially appropriate for his age.

The people who are most likely to notice are the child's contemporaries, and as a result, his peers often reject him. With his peers, such a child often stands out as clearly different. Some are victimized and bullied. They often have a high profile because of their inappropriate behavior. It is common for such children to be known by everyone in the school, but to have no friends.

Lack of friendship may make the child behave in an even more inappropriate way in order to gain attention. This is often the reason why such children will play the part of the 'class clown' or engage in provocative or eccentric behavior.

Specific social competence deficits

'Social cognition deficit' describes deficits in a number of areas of social incompetence. A child with ADHD may have one or more specific deficits. These include:

'Social blindness'

A 'socially blind' child has difficulty in reading a social situation so that behavior can be adapted accordingly.

Children with this difficulty do not pick up the same social cues as other children of the same age. For example, they are likely to rush in to a social group and start talking when it is clear that the group should be approached in a quiet manner, and that they should watch, wait, and listen first.

Egocentricity

It is a characteristic of young children that they tend to be very self-centered. Children with ADHD who have a social cognition defect will often behave in an egocentric way that is immature for their age. This will show itself in 'bossiness' with their peers. They want to dictate which games are played and insist on making, and often changing, the rules. They lack the degree of give-and-take that is appropriate for a child of their age.

Lack of appropriate inhibition

As normal children get older, they become more self-conscious and acutely aware of the need to behave in an appropriate manner for their age. Children with ADHD may not develop such awareness and remain uninhibited. They may undress in public without the embarrassment that their peers would experience. They may be over-friendly to strangers. They may kiss classmates at an age when this is no longer appropriate. They may touch peers in a way that is not appropriate. None of these behaviors is carried out with any malice, but they evoke strong negative reactions. Some children with ADHD make unusual sounds in public, such as imitating animal noises, in order to attract attention. This may irritate their peers.

Insatiability

This behavior describes the tendency of children with ADHD to behave in a certain manner without knowing when to stop. Such a child will be clearly differentiated from his peers who do know when 'enough is enough'.

Insensitivity to style and convention

Children with ADHD are often not aware of those things that are considered essential for acceptance by their peer group. They may not notice appropriate dress or speech. They will then appear to be eccentric.

Children of a particular age generally use certain slang words and specific ways of expressing themselves that constitute 'child speak'. Children with ADHD may have difficulty learning age-appropriate 'child-speak' and may speak, instead, in a way that sets them apart from other children of their age. They may not be as quick as other children in adapting to changes in style, so that they are still wearing last year's fashion when their peers have discarded it.

Lack of responsiveness

Many children with ADHD are incapable of being receptive to other children's social initiatives. This is due to their egocentricity that makes them unable to subjugate their own desires in order to take the desires of others into account.

Over-talkativeness

Because of their impulsivity and social immaturity, many children with ADHD have great difficulty being quiet. When they are anxious in a social group they become particularly talkative. Such garrulousness is quickly picked up by other children as being abnormal. It also means that the child is often very self-disclosing, talking about his own feelings and vulnerabilities, and this may encourage other children to bully and victimize him when they sense his weakness.

Poor metalinguistic skills

A particularly important area of development in children of school age is in the area of metalinguistic skills. This is the ability to analyze and reflect on language itself. Children with difficulties in this area will not be as competent as their peers in understanding metaphors, idioms, riddles, puns, jokes, and many other linguistic devices and nuances. Children with difficulties in this area will not be able to keep up with their more sophisticated peers. They will not understand jokes and may respond very literally to the things that their peers say.

Difficulties reading facial expression

Children with ADHD often have great difficulty 'reading' facial expressions and may be oblivious to whether someone is angry or upset with them. They may therefore not modify their behavior according to another person's response.

Recent research involving normal teenagers has shown that facial expressions are interpreted in the frontal lobes of the brain, the part that does not function normally in individuals with ADHD.

Aggressive tendencies

As children get older, they are more likely to resolve conflicts peacefully. Children with ADHD, particularly those with oppositional disorder, tend to resort to verbal or physical violence when frustrated. They lack the normal aptitude for settling a disagreement amicably. This makes them unpopular.

Lack of judgement

Children with ADHD may get themselves into all kinds of problems because of a lack of judgment. Often they will fight with children who are clearly larger and stronger than they are. They may try to establish friendships with children who actually dislike them and whom they should leave alone; or they will persist in annoying another child to the point where they will receive a negative response from the whole group.

Poor understanding of group dynamics

Many children with ADHD will manage well playing with one child at home. However, in the playground, where children often group together, they will have great difficulty. This may be because of difficulties with understanding group dynamics. Relating to other children as part of a group requires a subtle understanding of human relationships that is extremely difficult for a child with this kind of social cognitive deficit.

Pacing difficulties

Many children with ADHD have great difficulties knowing when to do or say things, and are often too quick in their timing and staging of social interactions and activities.

Misinterpreting feedback

Children with ADHD may misunderstand the cues that they are receiving from their peers. They may be insensitive to whether they are receiving negative or positive social feedback when relating to other children.

Tactlessness

Children with ADHD are often very tactless. Without intending any harm they will blurt out inappropriate or hurtful statements. They are unable to understand that things should not be said in certain situations. Because of their difficulties in predicting outcomes, they are often very surprised by the negative reaction that their behavior evokes. Sometimes they do not even notice other people's disapproval or hurt.

Poor social prediction

Children with ADHD have great difficulties predicting the consequences of their actions. They typically have little or no insight into how differently they are perceived. Unfortunately, this makes it very difficult for them to learn the skills that are required to mix with other children.

Poor social memory

The lack of the ability to recall prior social experience makes it difficult for children with ADHD to benefit from past experience.

Lack of awareness of image

Children with ADHD will often not be able to present themselves to peers in a socially acceptable way because they are unable to see themselves as their peers view them.

Poor behavior modification strategies

It is important for children to be able to understand and reinforce the feelings of their friends. Children with ADHD often have difficulty with this because they are not in tune with their peers' feelings and lack the strategies for reinforcing responses.

Lack of correction strategies

To make things more difficult, children with ADHD often have poor recuperative strategies to compensate for their social errors. Any child may make an error in social interaction, but most will then be able to compensate for this. Children with ADHD have difficulties in this area and may, in an attempt to correct things, further compound their difficulties.

Management of social clumsiness

Children with a social cognitive defect have a part of their brain that is immature relative to their peers. They would like to be liked and socially successful, but they do not yet have the ability to learn the necessary techniques.

It is all too easy to believe that helping a child with a social cognitive defect is simply a matter of teaching new strategies. It has to be realized that in many children with ADHD one is dealing with a brain that is not yet ready to learn these strategies.

No amount of social skills training will help a child to behave in a socially appropriate way if he is not yet ready to understand and, more importantly, apply such skills. It is characteristic of children with this sort of difficulty that they may be able to behave in an appropriate way in a very structured social skills group, but then have difficulty applying such behavior in their day-to-day interactions.

Wherever possible, parents should try to help the child by modifying the environment in which he finds himself. Occasionally a change of school may be helpful; however, because the problems lie with the child, difficulties with social relationships may reappear in the new setting.

Parents may need to take an active role in arranging for another child to play with their child after school. Parents can also play a role by tactfully pointing out ways in which the child could win friends. It may be helpful to rehearse certain situations with your child so that he learns how to act in them. This should be done so that it is an enjoyable experience.

It is important to try to identify which particular aspects of social interaction are causing difficulties. For example, a child with difficulties understanding dress styles and with a poor awareness of his image may need the parent to keep an eye on appropriate fashions and to ensure that he is dressed in a way that blends in with his peers.

Some health centers and adolescent units run social skills training groups where children of all ages learn to better understand the social consequences of their actions. They can also acquire techniques for interpreting social cues and for being accepted by their peers.

Cognitive training may also be helpful. In this form of therapy, the child is given one-to-one counseling by a professional trained in social skills development. The child can be taught techniques, such as to stop and think before acting. He is taught to first stop, then to focus and look at the possible ways he may act, and then, thirdly, to act according to a plan. The child is taught, lastly, to evaluate what has happened. Children who are well motivated may respond to this sort of help.

Medication can be extremely helpful to a child with a social cognition defect and may be used alone or in conjunction with other treatment. The medicines used for ADHD will often improve behaviors that impair social relationships, such as disinhibition, impulsivity, garrulousness, and aggressive tendencies. Children with ADHD are rated more positively by their peers when they are on medication.

Asperger syndrome

The social cognition deficits described above can cause significant difficulties for a child with ADHD. However, in a small proportion of children with ADHD, their social difficulties are too severe to be explained by ADHD alone. Such a child may have an additional condition.

An important cause of social impairment that may co-exist with ADHD is Asperger syndrome. This syndrome is associated with ADHD more often than would be explained by chance alone. This association (co-morbidity) occurs because the two conditions share a number of causative genes. The phenomenon of co-morbidity in ADHD is explained in Chapter 1 and the genetic aspects of this are explained in Chapter 10.

Historical background

The syndrome was named after Dr Hans Asperger, an Austrian psychiatrist. The word 'syndrome' refers to a cluster of features that 'run' together (*syn* = 'together'; *dromos* = 'track').

Asperger first described the condition in a paper published in 1944. He was interested in identifying why some children were not attracted to the Nazi youth movement. He identified children, mainly boys, who had difficulty mixing with their peers, did not enjoy group activities, and were eccentric and aloof in their behavior. He regarded their behavior as a mild form of autism.

Asperger's paper was not widely read in the English-speaking world because it was published in German during the Second World War. It was not until the 1990s that the syndrome gained worldwide acceptance as a developmental disorder.

Alternative names

Asperger syndrome is sometimes known by other names. Professionals from different disciplines may use a term that derives from their particular perspective of the child's disability. Speech therapists often use the term 'semantic-pragmatic disorder'. 'Semantics' refers to the meaning of words, 'pragmatics' to the social use of communication. Educational psychologists may use the term 'non-verbal learning disorder', emphasizing the difficulties with non-verbal learning. Psychiatrists, who view Asperger syndrome as a mild form of autism, may use the terms 'high-functioning autism' or 'pervasive developmental disorder (NOS)'. The abbreviation 'NOS' stands for 'Not Otherwise Specified'.

Parents who are told that their child has any of these conditions should check if the professional who makes the diagnosis is using a synonym for Asperger syndrome. Using a different term may make it difficult for both parents and professionals to access appropriate help and information.

How the diagnosis is made

There is no test for Asperger syndrome. Checklists of the characteristic features are useful, but do not replace the opinion of an experienced professional. The diagnosis should be made by a developmental pediatrician or a child psychiatrist.

The diagnosis of Asperger syndrome is not always an easy one to make. Sometimes the features are not evident when the child is young and become apparent with the passage of time. Many normal children have some degree of eccentricity and difficulty understanding social cues. These problems do not necessarily imply that a child has Asperger syndrome.

The basic deficit

Children normally develop the concept that other people have minds of their own and become able to understand the way another person may be thinking. They are therefore able to appreciate and predict how someone else may respond in a particular situation. This concept of other people's minds is known as a 'theory of mind'.

A child with Asperger syndrome does not have a well-developed theory of mind. He will not be able to put himself in someone else's position and appreciate how they may be thinking. This makes other people's behavior puzzling and unpredictable to a child with the syndrome.

To understand the concept of a theory of mind, an example may be helpful:

A child is shown a series of pictures. The first picture shows a covered box and a covered basket standing side by side. In the next picture a girl is seen placing a ball in the basket before replacing the cover—she then leaves. In the next picture, while the girl is away, a boy appears and moves the ball from the basket to the box. He replaces the covers before departing. In the last picture the girl, shown in the early pictures, returns.

The child who has examined the pictures is then asked the question, 'Where will the girl look for the ball?'. A child with a theory of mind will put himself in the girl's place and appreciate that she is unaware that the ball was moved while she was away. He will choose the basket as the place where she will look because it was there that she placed it.

A child without a theory of mind will not be able to see the situation from the girl's perspective; he will expect her to look for the ball in the box because *he* knows that that is where it is.

This example should not be used to test whether a child has Asperger syndrome (many children with the syndrome have a competent enough theory of mind to manage this simple problem)—it is quoted to illustrate the nature of the difficulties that children with the syndrome face.

Features

Asperger syndrome is characterized by severe social cognition difficulties as well as a restricted range of interests and activities. Not every child with the syndrome will have all the features of the condition.

Poor social skills

The child's social interactions with his peers are poor. He may make little eye contact when talking to another person. His interactions may lack reciprocity (give-and-take). His facial expression may be unvaried with little indication of emotion. He may not be able to make his wishes known with his eyes alone.

He may be a 'loner' showing little spontaneous enjoyment in interacting with others. He may be unaware of the feelings and needs of others. His social relationships may be one-sided and his perspective egocentric. He may show little emotion in many situations.

Unusual speech

His speech may be stilted and pedantic—as if he is giving a lecture. He may speak about his own interests with little insight into whether he has chosen an appropriate time and whether the listener is interested. His voice may be monotonous—lacking normal inflexions. The voice of a child with the syndrome is often loud and high.

He may be very literal in his understanding and fail to appreciate humor or figures of speech. He may speak about himself in the third person and may use certain words in an idiosyncratic way.

Tactile defensiveness

He may not like to be touched or he may tolerate being cuddled only on his own terms without returning the affection.

Increased and decreased sensitivity

Some children with the syndrome are over-sensitive to loud sounds, lights, and odors.

Others have reduced sensitivity to cold and pain. They may insist on wearing inadequate clothing in cold weather. When hurt, they may not seek assistance or comfort.

Poor self-awareness

A child with Asperger syndrome may be indifferent to what other children think of him, never showing embarrassment despite his inappropriate behavior in front of his peers. Even when taught appropriate behavior, he may apply what he has learned in a 'rote' and stilted way.

Clumsiness and mannerisms

Children with the syndrome are often awkward—their gestures large and ungainly.

A child with Asperger syndrome may rock, fidget, or pace around when concentrating. When excited he may display mannerisms such as running on his toes, moving back and forth in one spot, or flapping his hands.

Restricted range of interests and activities

He may be very attached to a particular object and refuse to be parted from it even when going out.

He may repeat the same pattern of behavior for long periods of time each day. Such behavior may be purposeless (e.g. switching appliances on and off), or may be purposeful but excessive (e.g. watching the same video repeatedly for hours on end).

Inflexibility

He may not tolerate change in his routine. His inflexibility may also extend to what he wears and what he eats. He may be fixated on a particular subject and speak about little else.

Over-reactions to teasing

The eccentric behavior, naivety, and gullibility of children with Asperger syndrome often lead to their being ostracized and bullied by other children. They may then become stressed and over-react, perhaps lashing out with uncharacteristic aggression.

Asperger syndrome in adulthood

Asperger syndrome is a condition that has only recently been widely recognized. It is a label that is used to describe individuals with a wide range of ability. It is therefore impossible to predict accurately how a specific child with the condition will manage as an adult.

The special difficulties generally persist into adulthood although most individuals do become more competent socially as they mature into adults. Many adults with the syndrome excel in jobs in fields such as science and technology (e.g. computing) where a subtle understanding of inter-personal relationships is not required. They may also manage very well in adult social settings where eccentricity is better tolerated than in childhood. They are much better in small social groups and may avoid large gatherings.

Management of Asperger syndrome

Although there is no specific treatment for Asperger syndrome, there is much that can be done to assist a child with this disorder. All the suggestions described above for the management of specific social competence deficits in ADHD may be applied to a child with Asperger syndrome. In addition, there are some special considerations:

It is important that the diagnosis be made so that the child's very significant difficulties are understood. This enables parents and professionals to adjust their expectations to take into consideration the child's disabilities and to gain a realistic appreciation of his special needs. The correct diagnosis also enables parents to access the considerable amount of information about the syndrome, as well as the special resources for supporting children with the syndrome. Information about assisting a child with Asperger syndrome may be obtained from books on the condition, internet sites devoted to the syndrome, and support groups for parents of children with the syndrome. Asperger syndrome is part of the autistic-spectrum disorders and so autistic associations may also provide information; however, it is important to realize that autistic disorder is a far more severe condition than Asperger syndrome and so any such information must be pertinent to the syndrome and not unique to other forms of autism.

A child with the syndrome may need to be taught to make eye contact, as this does not come naturally. A speech therapist may be able to help with this. Such a therapist may also help the child gain better skills in using language in an appropriate, interactive way. He or she may also assist the child to understand social conventions and the figurative use of language.

Children who have preoccupations or repetitive and ritualistic behaviors may need to be encouraged to spend their time in more socially appropriate, constructive, and varied ways. A psychologist or teacher trained in helping children with Asperger syndrome can be of great assistance in advising ways of doing this. It is important to let the child become used to change. Routines should be varied in a gradual way so as not to distress the child, while at the same time preventing him from becoming too used to routine and set in his ways. He also needs to be distracted away from his obsessions into more constructive activities.

Children with the syndrome are often very anxious and easily stressed. This is because they tolerate change so poorly and because other people's behavior is so often confusing to them. It is important to protect a child with the syndrome from being bullied or provoked by other children. Peers may need to be educated to understand the child's special difficulties and playtimes may need to be discreetly supervised.

If the child does over-react to stress, his behavior should be seen in perspective.

In addition to measures to protect the child from unnecessarily stressful experiences, some children with Asperger syndrome benefit from medication to reduce anxiety and stress. Tranquilizers should not be used for this purpose as their effect wears off with time, they make the child less alert and therefore less able to learn, and they may be habit-forming. However, medicines from the group known as SSRIs (Selective Serotonin Re-uptake Inhibitors) are often very effective in reducing anxiety and obsessional behavior. They are not sedating or habit-forming. The effect of SSRI medicines does not wear off with time.

Another group of medicines known as 'atypical antipsychotics' (e.g. risperidone) can also be extremely effective, but they do have many potential side effects that need to be discussed with the child's doctor. They can cause sedation and their effect may decrease over time. Risperidone is discussed in Chapter 16.

An appropriate school placement is essential for a child with Asperger syndrome. Some schools are better than others at adapting to the special needs of a child with the syndrome. A smaller school with smaller classes is usually best. The teachers and principal must be understanding with a positive attitude and a preparedness to take advice from expert consultants. The involvement of a psychologist to advise the teachers is very helpful.

In some educational systems the school can apply for special funding to assist in the provision of extra assistance to a pupil with Asperger syndrome. A supporting letter confirming the diagnosis and outlining the child's special needs may be required from the child's doctor.

9 Emotional disorders

In the descriptions of ADHD published over the past one hundred years, the behavioral problems associated with the disorder were the first to be recognized. The learning difficulties were identified some 50 years later, and the emotional disorders were only appreciated more recently. This is understandable because the emotional disorders in children with ADHD are often difficult to detect. There are a number of reasons for this.

First, a child's behavior may hide her emotional state. For example, a child with ADHD may be outwardly aggressive and overpowering and yet inwardly anxious and depressed.

Second, children with ADHD rarely have insight into their feelings and are generally unable or unwilling to discuss these. In fact, their low self-esteem may make them deny their true feelings if they regard them as evidence of vulnerability.

Third, the emotional state of children with ADHD often changes as they grow older. For example, a child may develop depression for the first time during adolescence. In such a situation, her worsening mood may be wrongly attributed to the ADHD and the child's depression overlooked.

It is, therefore, essential to be aware of the frequent occurrence of emotional disorders in children with ADHD. If you do suspect that your child has such a disorder, you should raise your concerns with your child's doctor as early as possible. While a book, such as this one, can be helpful, there is no substitute for an experienced doctor who knows your child first hand.

The emotional problems that occur in children with ADHD fall into three categories: emotional characteristics of ADHD, reactive emotions to having ADHD, and co-existing emotional disorders.

Emotional characteristics of ADHD

Children with ADHD may have emotional problems that are an integral component of their ADHD. Inefficient inhibitory processes in the brain are the basis of these emotional difficulties. This is analogous to the role of inhibitory failure in the causation of other aspects of the condition. The emotional problems are due to failure of inhibitory mechanisms to suppress certain thoughts and feelings in the same way that the impulsivity is due to their failure to suppress instantaneous reactions, and the poor concentration is due to their failure to suppress extraneous stimuli.

Common emotional characteristics of ADHD are low frustration tolerance, preoccupations, thrill-seeking, moodiness, and over-excitability:

Low frustration tolerance

Children with ADHD often cannot control their feelings like other children of the same age. Their thoughts, and therefore their actions, are impacted upon by strong emotions to a far greater degree than their peers. This means that such children may have uncontrollable rages that are disproportionate to the triggering event. When these children feel under stress, or when their desires are thwarted, they become overwhelmed by anger and explode.

Such outpourings of rage are frightening to observers and, often, to the child herself. The outburst can continue for many hours with the child hurling abuse, making threats, and acting out her anger physically against objects and people.

This physical aggression can be directed towards anyone or anything that the child comes across—even uninvolved bystanders. The child will even damage or destroy her own prized possessions in such an 'affective storm', as such episodes are known.

The child may behave in this way in the company of strangers without showing any embarrassment. The feeling of rage often overwhelms the child to such a degree that she will be in tears during the outburst. Many children run away or hide during or after such episodes.

Some children will be depressed and ashamed afterwards and apologize. Some will cover such feelings of shame with displays of bravado. Other children will not remember anything that happened during an episode.

Such episodes are so severe that observers may question whether the child has had some form of seizure. While a particular form of epilepsy, (temporal lobe epilepsy) can cause rage episodes, these occur out of the blue with no provocation. In the rages associated with ADHD, however, the trigger may be small but it is always present.

Preoccupations

Children with ADHD usually cannot filter out thoughts and emotions as easily as other children. Thoughts infect their minds, like a computer virus, and cannot be dislodged. The sensation is similar to that which occurs when one has been staring at a bright light and the image of the light remains imprinted on the retina after turning away.

The child cannot erase thoughts or worries from her mind. She will find it hard to relax during the day and difficult to fall asleep at night because her mind is so active.

For a similar reason, a child with ADHD will often nag interminably for something she wants. If there is something she is interested in, she may become obsessed with it and think of nothing else. She will accept no limits to her preoccupation and may want her parents to spend vast amounts of money on acquisitions connected with this passion. She will feel that they are being unreasonable if they refuse to do so.

Older children with ADHD who have access to their own money may squander large amounts on acquisitions related to their area of interest. Such insatiability and over-focusing are common features of ADHD.

It may seem strange that a condition that is characterized by poor concentration should be associated with 'over-focusing'. However, this type of paradoxical 'overfocusing' is in reality a form of persistent 'over-distraction' in which the child's inability to shift her attention normally from one matter to another allows persistent distracting preoccupations to constantly invade her thoughts.

Eventually the overwhelming preoccupation comes to an abrupt end and the child shows no further interest in what once consumed her. Frequently, after a short interval, a new preoccupation appears.

This preoccupation must be distinguished from obsessive-compulsive disorder that is described below. In obsessive-compulsive disorder, unlike the preoccupations seen as part of ADHD, the obsessions are more repetitive, ritualistic, and pointless.

Thrill seeking

Children with the hyperactive-impulsive and combined types of ADHD often have faulty novelty and desire mechanisms in their brains that lead them to thrill-seeking behavior regardless of the danger. This is discussed further in the next chapter.

An element of danger may need to be present for an activity to be enjoyed by some children with ADHD. Risk-taking behavior is therefore more common in children with these types of ADHD.

This puts them at a greater risk of substance abuse. The most commonly abused substances are cigarettes, alcohol, and marijuana. One of the positive aspects of treating ADHD with medication is that research has shown that this substantially decreases the risk of later substance abuse. This is described in Chapter 16.

Dysthymia

Many children with ADHD have a constant feeling of dissatisfaction with life that is not severe enough to be regarded as depression. They seem to be 'down in the dumps' most of the time. Such children fail to derive pleasure from any activity or experience. They frequently complain that everything is 'boring' and that 'it sucks' and they hardly ever smile or laugh. They are often reluctant to embark on any new activity claiming that they know they will not enjoy themselves. This state is known as 'dysthymia'.

Children with dysthymia are often moody and irritable. They tend to be at their worst in the early morning when they are often groggy and uncooperative. It is characteristic of dysthymia that this mood persists for most of the day.

The possibility that this morning grogginess and moodiness is due to a sleep disorder should always be considered. Children with morning moodiness who also snore and breathe irregularly or noisily in their sleep may need special tests to detect whether they have obstruction to the back of the nose and the throat during sleep (obstructive sleep apnoea). If present, this is usually caused by conditions such as enlarged adenoids and tonsils. Obstructive sleep apnoea leads to disturbed sleep that may be the cause of the morning moodiness rather than the ADHD.

A child should also not be regarded as having dysthymia unless an assessment to rule out depression has been performed.

Over-excitability

Dysthymia, because of its effect on mood, deprives some children with ADHD of enthusiasm for enjoyable experiences. However, some children with ADHD have the opposite problem—they have a tendency to become overexcited and difficult to control when enjoying themselves. This is a manifestation of the impulsivity that is common in ADHD.

When children with over-excitability are enjoying themselves they become so overwhelmed by their feelings that their behavior becomes inappropriate and difficult to control. They lose the ability to behave in a responsible manner and often show off in an extreme way, take risks, become defiant and challenging, and even aggressive. The episode often ends in tears. Those who know the child may be surprised by how bizzare the child's behavior becomes in such a situation.

A typical situation in which this kind of behavior is seen occurs when a friend comes to play. Sometimes parents are forced to stop certain treats because they end so disastrously for all concerned.

Reactive emotions

As a result of their condition, children with ADHD have to contend with many difficulties and disappointments. The impact that these have on their self-esteem may give rise to a number of emotional responses. These responses, and their related behaviors, comprise the second category of emotional disorders that occur in children with ADHD. They are described in detail in Chapter 7 and so are not discussed further in this chapter.

Co-existing (co-morbid) emotional disorders

Children with ADHD are more likely to suffer from certain specific emotional disorders than other children. This tendency for two conditions to co-exist is known as co-morbidity. In this case, the co-morbidity occurs because the two conditions, the ADHD and the emotional disorder, share common genes and so are commonly associated. This is described further in the next chapter.

A co-morbid emotional disorder may develop at any time in a child's life although this most commonly occurs at puberty. The deterioration in the child's condition may be incorrectly attributed to the hormonal changes of puberty, the child's increase in size outstripping her dose of medication, or to some other change in the child's life.

It is not uncommon for a child with ADHD to change at adolescence from having ADHD as her sole disorder to having another condition, such as depression or obsessive-compulsive disorder, as her major or sole problem.

This sequence may lead to the erroneous belief that the original diagnosis of ADHD was incorrect—that the child had actually been suffering from the emotional disorder all along and that this had been mistaken for ADHD. However this common sequence does not imply that the first diagnosis was incorrect.

A child with ADHD who has a co-morbid emotional disorder may require special treatment for the disorder (counseling with or without medication). It is therefore important that those who care for children with ADHD should be alert to the possibility that a co-morbid emotional disorder may develop.

Unfortunately, the occurrence of a co-morbid disorder may mean that a child with ADHD needs to take more than one medication: one for the ADHD and another for the emotional disorder. Parents are often alarmed when their child's doctor suggests an additional medicine, but one medication is unlikely to help both ADHD and the associated emotional disorder.

Frequently, the co-morbid disorder starts at a time that the ADHD is resolving and it may then be possible to withdraw the medication used to treat the ADHD and replace it with one used to treat the co-morbid emotional disorder.

Specific co-morbid emotional disorders

Depression

Depression is significantly more common in children with ADHD. It is characterized by intense feelings of sadness and lack of pleasure in any activity.

A depressed child may become withdrawn and avoid contact with her family and friends. She may lack energy and everything may be too much of an effort. She may spend large amounts of time sitting in front of the television or lying on her bed. She may eat and sleep poorly. She may appear dejected, as if about to burst into tears. She may experience feelings of worthlessness and guilt. She may be very negative about herself and very sensitive to any perceived criticism by others. Depressed children usually cry easily.

Occasionally a child who is depressed becomes irritable rather than sad.

A child with depression may feel that her life is not worth living and some have suicidal thoughts and may even attempt suicide.

Depression must always be treated with concern because of the risk of suicide. The child will benefit from counseling. Life style changes also help and it has been shown that children who exercise cope better with depression. Medication for depression can be very helpful if used in conjunction with counseling.

Anxiety disorder

Anxiety disorder is approximately five times more common in children with ADHD. It is characterized by intense worry that cannot be controlled by the child. She may talk about her fearful feelings, or her anxiety may be expressed in bodily symptoms such as cold and clammy hands, a 'lump in the throat', a racing heart, abdominal discomfort, and diarrhoea. The anxiety may be constant or episodic. Sometimes acute episodes of extreme anxiety are experienced (panic attacks).

The disorder may take the form of generalized anxiety disorder in which worrisome thoughts are free-floating and attach themselves to one thing after another. A child with this disorder will be a worrier who is constantly concerned about what lies ahead. Nothing seems straightforward to such a child; an imagined catastrophe is always about to happen. Such a child is often a perfectionist. She may re-do her work because of her dissatisfaction with anything less than perfection. A child with anxiety disorder is generally very insecure and will constantly seek reassurance about her performance. Unfortunately, no amount of reassurance or positive experience dispels her fearfulness.

In some children, their anxiety is confined to certain specific situations. This kind of intense fear of a particular thing or situation is known as a phobia. Common phobias in children with anxiety disorder include school phobia (fear of attending school), social phobia (fear of being embarrassed in public), and separation anxiety (fear of being away from home).

Anxiety is best treated by counseling the child. With generalized anxiety the child can benefit from learning relaxation techniques and from cognitive therapy, where the child learns more positive ways of thinking (mind over body). Children with phobias may benefit from desensitization, in which the child is helped to cope with fearful situations in a gradual step-wise process.

Tranquilizers do not have a place in the treatment of anxiety as they lose their potency with time, make children less alert, and can be habit-forming. However, there are newer medicines from the SSRI (Selective Serotonin Reuptake Inhibitors) class of medicines, that can be effective in generalized anxiety if used in conjunction with counseling.

The dose of the medicine used to treat the child's ADHD may need to be slightly lower than usual when co-morbid anxiety disorder is present. Normal doses may aggravate the anxiety. Often the anxiety tends to diminish when the child's ADHD is treated with medication.

Obsessive-compulsive disorder

Obsessive-compulsive disorder is approximately five times more common in children with ADHD. It is characterized by the presence of time-consuming obsessions and/or compulsions.

Obsessions are persistent thoughts that are intrusive and inappropriate and cause distress to a child. They are not within her control.

Compulsions are repetitive behaviors, such as hand washing or counting backwards, that the child carries out in order to reduce her feelings of distress. She feels driven to perform the compulsion in order to prevent some dreaded outcome. Compulsions may be simple or elaborate. The child will become very distressed if someone stops her from performing her compulsion.

Obsessive-compulsive disorder often responds to counseling that teaches the child to control her thoughts (cognitive therapy). Medicines from the SSRI class, which are also used to treat depression, are very helpful in obsessive-compulsive disorder, but are best used in conjunction with counseling.

Bipolar disorder

Bipolar disorder is more common in adolescents and adults with ADHD. It is rare in younger children.

Bipolar disorder is characterized by the occurrence of one or more 'manic episodes'. This term describes a change in mood lasting several days or more, when the individual becomes abnormally euphoric.

A manic episode is not to be confused with a healthy feeling of happiness or exuberance, but is an alarming and excessive state of mind that will be recognized by those who know the individual as quite out of character. The adolescent will seem to be out of control, on an extraordinary 'high'—as if she has taken a drug that has altered her mind and affected her judgment. She will have increased energy and hardly sleep, her speech will be rapid and voluble and her thoughts will race in a chaotic way. She will display an inflated opinion of her own importance and show poor judgment, for example telephoning the school principal at home and telling him or her how she thinks the school should be run. She will display poor judgment, becoming reck-lessly involved in unrestrained behaviors to satisfy her own pleasure, such as spending money (her own or her parents') on extravagant pur-chases, or becoming sexually promiscuous.

Manic episodes are often associated with episodes of depression, and some individuals may move from one extreme to the other.

The opinion of a child psychiatrist should be sought as a matter of urgency in the case of an adolescent who is experiencing a manic episode. There are now a number of mood stabilizing medicines (including lithium, valproate, and carbemazepine) that can be used to control a manic episode and prevent recurrences.

Section 3

The cause of ADHD

10
An impairment in brain function

There is a tendency to attribute all difficulties that children have in learning or behavior to 'bad parenting', or to some 'attitudinal' problem on the part of the child.

These ways of explaining children's difficulties arise from a number of traditions. First, people have for generations used terms such as 'naughty', 'lazy', and 'spoilt' without thinking carefully about the origins of children's behavioral and learning difficulties. Such phrases are handed down from parent to child as folk wisdom.

Second, the writings of Sigmund Freud, which have greatly influenced the thinking of many lay people and professionals, largely interpret children's behavior in the light of their early experiences.

Third, many psychologists now practicing were trained by behaviorists, who emphasize that behavior is learned. Behaviorism is based on research involving laboratory animals and the work of scientists such as Pavlov and Skinner.

The belief that behavior is determined *exclusively* by external factors is no longer tenable. There is a great deal of evidence that children's brains are not 'blank slates' and that differences in brain development, structure, and function can give rise to behavioral and learning problems that are not a consequence of the environment.

Most important has been the realization that, in order to help many children with learning and behavioral difficulties, we may need to treat the basic impairment of the brain function. It is now recognized that for such children, treatment with counseling and behavioral training *alone* is often doomed to fail. ADHD is such a disorder.

The proof that ADHD is a brain disorder, and not simply a matter of inappropriate child rearing or unrealistic expectations of children's learning and behavior, comes from four areas of scientific research.

This research has also provided our understanding of how ADHD comes about.

Executive function deficits

In the 1970s the Canadian psychologist, Virginia Douglas, demonstrated that children with ADHD attained significantly lower scores on objective tests that measured attentional ability compared to normal children of the same age. Since that time a great deal of research has been carried out testing various cognitive abilities, such as working memory, sequencing, and impulse control, in children with ADHD and comparing their performance to that of normal children. These studies have consistently shown that there are significant measurable deficits in certain cognitive abilities in children with ADHD.

Children with ADHD have deficits in specific brain functions known as the 'executive functions'. These are described in the section 'Executive functions'.

Frontal lobe under-activity

A type of brain scan, called a PET scan (Positron Emission Tomography), shows which part of the brain is active (i.e., utilizing glucose and oxygen) at any one time. When normal individuals carry out executive functions the frontal lobes become very active.

The earliest PET studies carried out in people with ADHD were those by Hans Lou in Denmark (children) and Alan Zemetkin in the USA (adults). These studies demonstrated that the frontal regions (particularly a part known as the 'striatal area') of these individuals were less active than those of normal subjects when they were carrying out executive functions.

The parts of the brain involved in ADHD are discussed in the section 'The frontal lobes of the brain'.

Neurotransmitter depletion

Hans Lou showed that the abnormalities on the PET scans of children with ADHD were corrected when a medicine, methylphenidate (Ritalin), was given. Ritalin increases the levels of a chemical messenger (neurotransmitter) known as 'dopamine' that is produced at the ends of nerve cells in certain parts of the brain.

Dopamine levels in the living brain cannot be measured directly. However, a revolutionary technique has made indirect measurement possible. This is due to the development of small chemical molecule, 'altropane', that binds avidly and specifically to the part of nerve cells where dopamine is reabsorbed after use. This is known as the 'dopamine transporter'. Altropane can be radioactively labeled and measured in the brain using special scans.

Measurement of altropane has shown that there is 70% more dopamine transporter activity in the frontal area of the brains of many individuals with ADHD compared to normal individuals. In many individuals with ADHD, therefore, dopamine is being recycled before it has had chance to do its work as a chemical messenger. This and other neurotransmitter abnormalities in ADHD are discussed in the section 'Neurotransmitters'.

Gene defects

There is a great deal of evidence that genetic factors are important in the causation of ADHD. First, there is an increased frequency of ADHD in the relatives of individuals with the disorder. Second, studies of adopted children of parents with ADHD have demonstrated an increased frequency of ADHD in these children despite their being raised away from their biological parents. Third, there are a number of large studies of identical and non-identical twins that demonstrate that genetic factors are paramount. This information is obtained by comparing a measure known as the 'concordance rate'.

'Concordance' means that both of a pair of twins is the same with respect to the condition studied (i.e. if one has ADHD, the other twin also has it, or if one does not have it, the other twin also does not have it). If concordance rates for identical and non-identical twins are no different then a condition is caused only by factors in the child's environment, such as the way the child was raised.

In ADHD the concordance rate for identical twins is extremely high, while for non-identical twins it is the same as for non-twin siblings. This demonstrates that the genetic component in the causation of ADHD is extremely high.

The figures obtained from concordance rate studies can be used to calculate the exact contribution made by genes to the causation of a disorder. This is known as the hereditability factor and in ADHD this is approximately 95%. ADHD is therefore primarily a genetic disorder—the child's environment plays only a very small part in its causation.

Genetic studies have led to the identification of a number of defective genes associated with ADHD. All of these genes influence the amount of the neurotransmitters dopamine and norepinephrine (sometimes known as 'noradrenaline') available in nerves connected to the frontal lobes. Some of these genes are discussed in the section 'ADHD genes'.

Overview of causation

The four findings described above: executive function deficits, frontal lobe under-activity, neurotransmitter depletion, and genetic defects, allow the causation of ADHD to be traced from the basic problems with learning and behavior back to the genetic defects from which the condition originates.

The causation of ADHD is described in the five sections that follow. In the first section, 'executive functions', the basic nature of the impairment in brain processing in ADHD is outlined. In the second section, 'the frontal lobes', the part of the brain impaired in ADHD is described. The third section, 'neurotransmitters', describes the brain chemicals involved in ADHD. The fourth section deals with the genetic defects in ADHD. In the last section, the changes that occur at puberty and some of the non-genetic factors that may contribute to causation are discussed.

Executive functions

The human brain is an organ of breathtaking complexity. Its information processing power dwarfs even that of the most powerful man-made super-computers. The brain must deal appropriately with a steady stream of information from the outside world as well as the flow of thoughts and feelings that originate within the mind itself. A huge range of responses is available to the brain, from the simplest twitch of a muscle to complex tasks such as speaking and writing.

Like a large business organization, the brain carries out its tasks in an hierarchical system. Lower-order functions (such as talking, moving, seeing, and hearing) are carried out by the equivalent of the workers in the organization. Higher-order functions (such as self-organization, self-regulation, and self-appraisal) are carried out by the equivalent of the chief executive officer of the organization and are known as 'executive functions'.

The executive functions of the brain are listed in Table 4. These are functions such as concentration, reflection (stopping to think so as not to act impulsively), and social cognition ('reading' social situations in order to act appropriately). They enable an individual to plan ahead, defer gratification, and to modulate his mood. They play a vital role in controlling the individual's performance.

It is impairment of these executive functions that gives rise to the features of ADHD described in Chapter 1. In Table 5 each executive function is matched up to a corresponding feature of ADHD.

It is evident that ADHD is not a problem of ability (the 'workers' in the organization are not directly affected), but of performance consistency—the problems one would expect if an organization lacked effective leadership.

When the executive functions of the brain fail, the individual responds to the world in an unfocused, disorganized, impulsive, and

Table 4 Executive functions of the brain

Sustained attention	Self-appraisal
Reflection	Social cognition
Temporary immobilization	Compliance
Self-organization	Working memory
Self-regulation	Co-ordination of movement

Table 5 Executive functions of the brain with the corresponding features of ADHD

Executive function	Feature of ADHD
Sustained attention	Poor concentration
Reflection	Impulsivity
Temporary immobilization	Overactivity
Self-organization	Lack of planning
Self-regulation	Inflexibility
Self-appraisal	Poor self-esteem
Social cognition	Social clumsiness
Compliance	Defiant behavior
Working memory	Forgetfulness
Co-ordination of movement	Clumsiness

chaotic way. These are the characteristics of the behavior and learning of children with ADHD.

In normal individuals the executive functions have two important characteristics:

- They are *intrinsic*, i.e. they are not learned but develop spontaneously.
- They are *maturational*, i.e. they become more refined and reliable with age.

These characteristics are important in understanding the difficulties experienced by children with ADHD.

Not all skills are taught

Many of the skills that children develop are not taught to them. A classic example is walking. While walking is not an executive function, it provides an observable example of an intrinsic skill. Children do not receive 'walking lessons', their brains are pre-wired to enable walking to occur. They do not even need much practice: the Hopi Indians keep their infants strapped to a cradle-board for much of the first year of life, yet they experience no difficulty in learning to walk.

The intrinsic nature of walking is paralleled by all the executive functions. For example, children are not taught to concentrate, to sit still, or to become self-directed—their brains are pre-programmed to develop these skills.

Ages and stages

Intrinsic skills, like the executive functions, are maturational.

Walking serves as an observable example of a maturational skill. Some time between 9 and 18 months of age, a child's brain develops spontaneously to the point where walking becomes possible, and only then can the child walk. A child cannot walk before the nervous system has reached the necessary degree of maturity, and no amount of encouragement or training will make a child succeed prior to this time.

The *fundamental* difficulties experienced by children with ADHD, such as poor attention and poor self-organization, involve skills that, like walking, are maturational. As children grow older, these functions develop and performance in each of these areas becomes more consistent and reliable.

As normal children grow older, they spontaneously develop competence in those areas where children with ADHD experience difficulty. For example, normal children become more competent at concentrating as they grow older. When younger, they can only concentrate for short periods of time, and then only when they are very interested in something. As they develop, the attentional mechanism in their brains becomes more competent. They can concentrate on things that are not inherently so interesting, they can concentrate even when there are some distractions, and they can concentrate for the sake of some intangible goal to be realized far off in the future. Similarly, as children grow older, they can sit still for longer periods of time, they become more persistent with tasks, they become less impulsive, they become more flexible in their relationships, they can defer gratification; they can cope better with frustration. In all these ways they become more mature because of changes that occur in their brains.

The failure of children with ADHD to develop age-appropriate executive skills has very important consequences for learning and behavior. It means that a normal, intelligent child may differ markedly from his peers in the consistency with which he can learn and behave.

The best way to understand the difficulties of a child with ADHD is often to think of him as being like a younger child in those areas in which he is experiencing difficulty. The basic difficulty for the child with ADHD is that, when he needs to concentrate, to sit still, to understand social situations, he is doing so with brain mechanisms that are inefficient and immature. It is not that he cannot do these things at all. Rather, the problem is that, like a younger child, he cannot do these things as *consistently* as other children of the same age. It is this performance inconsistency, the 'Jekyll and Hyde' nature of children with ADHD, that is so confusing.

To understand this inconsistency, it is necessary to appreciate that a developmental skill is not attained suddenly. Rather, the child slowly becomes more and more consistent in his ability to perform a particular skill over time. The best way to explain this is to view skill acquisition as going through three stages.

The three stages of skill acquisition

Figure 2 shows a representation of the three stages of skill acquisition for walking.

Initially, the infant cannot walk at all—the stage of *incompetence* for this skill.

Next, he reaches a stage when he can take a few steps if supported, but quickly loses his balance. At this stage the child cannot walk

Figure 2 The three stages of skill acquisition for walking: incompetence (above left), inconsistency (above right), and competence (below).

quickly and becomes unstable if the terrain is not flat. This is the stage of *inconsistency* for this skill.

Eventually, his ability becomes more and more consistent and he becomes a competent walker. Now he does not tire easily, he can walk for long periods, and he remains stable on all kinds of terrain. He has reached the stage of *competence* for the skill.

For many developmental skills, the child with ADHD is stuck in the second stage of skill acquisition (inconsistency) when his contemporaries have already attained the stage of competence. Because he is delayed in his development, he remains in this stage for longer than usual. For example, when his peers can concentrate on tedious tasks for long periods (stage of competence for attention), he is still easily distracted unless the task is interesting (stage of inconsistency).

The performance inconsistency that children with ADHD experience will be better understood if this three-stage model is kept in mind.

The frontal lobes of the brain

The human brain differs in its functioning from the brains of other animals in the highly developed nature of its executive functions. Not surprisingly, the part of the brain where these functions are controlled forms a much larger proportion of the human brain than it does in the brains of other animals (for example 30% of the human brain, but only 3% of the cat's brain). This part of the brain, the frontal lobes, lies behind the forehead and is, from an evolutionary point of view, the most recently developed.

The frontal lobes form the 'command post' of the brain and are often likened to the conductor of an orchestra. Other parts of the brain are analogous to the instrumentalists, each with his or her own part to play—but it is the conductor who ensures that they play together in an integrated, purposeful, and balanced way.

The frontal lobes are situated at a pivotal position in the brain and communicate with every functional unit of the brain via a rich network of nerve pathways. No other part of the brain is so well connected. These lines of communication allow the frontal lobes to contain within them a 'map' of the rest of the brain. This is where the individual's inner perception, his consciousness of his mental world, resides.

A commander is only as good as his or her lines of communication and if the pathways connecting the frontal lobe to other parts of the brain are not able to function adequately, the ultimate outcome is no different to what would happen if the frontal lobes themselves were malfunctioning. In most individuals with ADHD it is the connecting pathways to and from the frontal lobes that function inadequately.

The commonest pathway to be affected is the 'fronto-striatal connection'. This links the frontal lobes to an area known as the 'striatum', which forms part of a group of structures at the base of the brain known as the 'basal ganglia'. The striatum is so called because of its striped appearance. It consists of two separate structures that lie side by side: an elongated 'caudate nucleus' and a rounded 'putamen'. In humans and in other mammals, the striatum works in such close collaboration with the frontal lobes that the frontal lobes and striatum together are referred to as 'the greater frontal lobes'. The frontal lobe and striatum are shown in Figure 3.

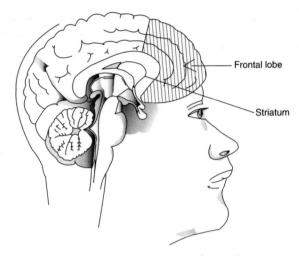

Figure 3 The frontal lobe and the location of the striatum.

A characteristic of the nerves forming the fronto-striatal connection is that they all produce the same family of chemical messengers to transmit impulses from one nerve cell to the next along the connection. This family of chemical messenger is known as the 'monoamines'. The particular monoamines involved in the nerves of this connection are 'dopamine' and 'norepinephrine'. Both of these monoamine neurotransmitters are involved in the causation of ADHD*.

When disruption to the fronto-striatal connection occurs, the executive functions fail. This has been well demonstrated in experimental animals. For example, when these areas of the brain are damaged in monkeys, they lose the ability to hoard nuts. The monkeys become unable to sustain attention on tasks that are not immediately rewarding and they cannot delay gratification. Unlike monkeys with intact frontal lobe connections, they consume all their nuts immediately as soon as they receive them. This is analogous to the impulsive behavior, poor forward planning, and lack of incentival motivation that are characteristic of individuals with the impulsive form of ADHD.

*A third monoamine neurotransmitter, serotonin, also plays a role in ADHD, but its role is less significant and so it is not discussed.

The greater frontal lobes also contain pleasure centers that depend on adequate levels of dopamine for stimulation. Without such stimulation, individuals cannot experience the pleasure of anticipation—they live for the moment[*]. As a result they may seek artificial ways to stimulate this area of the brain by using drugs of dependence that raise dopamine in this area (most addictive substances work in this way). This may explain the higher rates of substance abuse in untreated individuals with ADHD. When dopamine levels are normalized with medication, however, children with ADHD are less likely to seek addictive substances. This would explain why research has shown that individuals with ADHD who were treated with medication during childhood had significantly lower rates of both drug and substance dependence than those who were not.

Neurotransmitters

The brain is composed of a network of approximately 100 billion nerve cells. Each one of these nerve cells is linked to more than 1000 other nerve cells. Messages flow along nerves in a way that is comparable to low-voltage electricity traveling through wires.

The nerve cells end in long projections known as 'axons'. The electrical impulse comes to a stop at the end of the axon. The end of the axon does not touch the next nerve cell; it is separated from it by a small gap, the synapse. For the impulse to be transmitted to the next nerve it must traverse the synapse between adjoining nerve cells. A chemical messenger, the neurotransmitter, achieves this.

The neurotransmitter is released by the tip of the axon of the first nerve cell and crosses the synapse and attaches itself to a receptor on the next nerve cell. This stimulates the second cell to start an electrical impulse of its own. Figure 4 shows the end of a nerve cell (the axon tip) and the neurotransmitter it produces in order to transmit its message to the next nerve cell.

The production of the monoamine neurotransmitters, dopamine and norepinephrine, consists of a number of steps. The neurotransmitter must be manufactured in the cell from its basic components *(synthesis)*.

---

[*]*This condition has been referred to as the 'reward deficiency syndrome' and it is associated with abnormalities in dopamine pathways due to a defect in a particular dopamine controlling gene, the D2R2-receptor gene. Individuals with the abnormal gene have higher rates of substance abuse.*

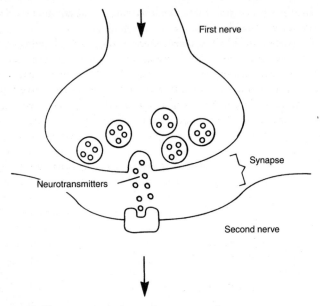

Figure 4 The synapse between two nerve cells.

It must then be stored in small containers in the cell, called the storage vesicles. When an electrical impulse reaches the end of the nerve cell, the neurotransmitter must be *released* from the nerve end. The neurotransmitter then exerts its action by attaching *(binding)* itself to a receptor on the next cell, causing it to fire (send a signal in turn).

Other factors also come into play. The amount of neurotransmitter present in the synapse will not only depend on the amount released by the nerve ending, but also on how quickly it is *broken down*, and thus inactivated, by enzymes present in the synapse.

There is a recycling process with the cell that manufactured the neurotransmitter, reabsorbing some of it so that it can be re-used *(re-uptake)*. In the case of dopamine, it is the dopamine transporter (DAT) that is responsible for this re-absorption.

There are also some feedback mechanisms that enable the cell to gauge whether there is sufficient neurotransmitter in the synapse or not. This is determined by autoreceptors on the nerve ending that produce the neurotransmitter. Any excess neurotransmitter in the synapse binds to the autoreceptors. If the *autoreceptors* are vacant, more neurotransmitter is released.

The receptor on which the neurotransmitter acts (by binding to it) must be responsive to it for transmission to occur. In the case of dopamine, there are five different types of receptor in normal individuals. Although dopamine itself can bind to any of these five types of receptor, medicines that affect dopamine receptors often work only on certain types of dopamine receptors and not on others. This makes the actions of many medicines specific to certain dopamine disorders.

This complex process of neurotransmitter production, release, reuptake, feedback control, and receptor binding is referred to as the 'metabolism of the neurotransmitter at the synapse'. The basic defect in ADHD is *faulty metabolism of dopamine and/or norepinephrine at the synapse* that leads to poor transmission of nerve impulses from one nerve to the next. Any stage in the metabolism of these neurotransmitters may be involved. For ADHD to occur, more than one stage is usually impaired, as will be explained in the next section.

The defects in ADHD are usually located in the nerve cells of the fronto-striatal connection. There is therefore effectively 'blockage' to nerve transmission in this part of the brain. When a message is required for adequate processing of an executive function, such as controlling impulsivity, concentrating, or for working with short-term memory, the message is not able to travel from one nerve cell to another. In the vast majority of individuals with ADHD, this comes about because of the presence of defective genes.

'ADHD genes'

All chemical processes in body cells are under the control of the genes. The metabolism of dopamine and norepinephrine neurotransmitters at the synapse is no exception. A separate gene controls each step in dopamine and norepinephrine metabolism at the synapse. There are literally hundreds of 'dopamine genes' and 'norepinephrine genes'. Some aspects of metabolism are common to dopamine and norepinephrine and so some genes affect both of these neurotransmitters.

A number of defective variants of dopamine and norepinephrine genes have been found to be associated with ADHD in studies carried out since the early 1990s. These variants are sometimes referred to as 'ADHD genes'.

Small numbers of these ADHD genes are not usually enough to cause significant disruption to dopamine or norepinephrine metabolism and to cause ADHD. This is because there are so many compensatory mechanisms in the metabolic pathways of these neurotransmitters at the synapse. For example, a reduction in dopamine release from the storage vesicles would be detected by the autoreceptor feedback mechanism, and dopamine levels would be maintained by an increase in dopamine synthesis and a reduction in dopamine re-uptake.

The presence of a small number of defective dopamine and norepinephrine genes is common in normal humans. It has been suggested that this may have come about because a degree of restlessness and impulsivity would have been advantageous during early human evolution. Individuals with these traits would have been more likely than their less adventurous companions to find new hunting and feeding grounds and to come across new sexual partners. This would have led to their having more offspring, many of whom would have received the defective neurotransmitter genes of their parents.

ADHD only occurs when *multiple disruptions* to dopamine and/or norepinephrine metabolism at the synapse by *several* ADHD genes overwhelms the compensatory mechanisms. It is the *additive effect* of these different genes that causes ADHD to occur. This is true whether all the defective genes present are dopamine genes, norepinephrine genes, or (as is often the case) defective genes for both neurotransmitters.

This additive effect leads to a significant disruption of nerve transmission that cannot be compensated by other steps in neurotransmitter metabolism. ADHD is therefore not a simple genetic disorder, caused by a single gene, but a complex 'polygenetic disorder' ('*poly*' comes from the Greek word for 'many').

Specific ADHD genes

A few examples of ADHD genes are listed in Table 6. The most studied of these genes are the dopamine D4 receptor gene (DRD4) and the dopamine transporter gene (DAT1). Individuals with ADHD are more likely to carry an abnormal variant of these genes.

The 'DRD4 gene' controls the formation of one of the five types of dopamine receptors (the D4 receptor). The gene variant associated with ADHD is longer than normal (a sequence on the gene is repeated 7 times, rather than the normal 2 or 4 times) resulting in a receptor that is less able to bind dopamine and therefore to respond to it. Not only has this gene been found to be far more common in children with ADHD,

Table 6 Some examples of 'ADHD genes'

Gene	Effect of the ADHD variant ('ADHD gene')
Dopamine transporter gene ('DAT1 gene')	Excessive re-absorption of dopamine by nerve
Dopamine receptor D4 gene ('DRD4 gene')	Blunted response to dopamine by receptor ('novelty-seeking gene')
Dopamine beta-hydroxylase	Decreased dopamine synthesis
DOPA decarboxylase gene	Reduced amount of dopamine stored in vesicles
Adrenergic$_{2A}$ receptor gene	Blunted response to norepinephrine by receptor

but it has also been associated with the behavioral trait of novelty seeking in humans. This is therefore a gene that plays a role in the impulsive type of ADHD, rather then inattentive type, and would explain the risk-taking behavior in many children with impulsive ADHD.

The dopamine transporter is responsible for re-absorption of dopamine into the cell from which it was released. This is an important area of dopamine metabolism because the transporter is the site where Ritalin, the main medication used in ADHD, works. Ritalin blocks the dopamine transporter, reducing dopamine re-uptake and so making more dopamine available in the synapse. The gene that controls the transporter is the 'DAT1' gene and the variant associated with ADHD has a longer than normal gene sequence (it is repeated 10 times). This variant has been shown to cause a 70% increase in dopamine transporter activity and to be associated with both the impulsive and the inattentive types of ADHD.

The research into the genetics of ADHD is very intensive at present and there is no doubt that a large number of new 'ADHD genes' will be identified over the next few years. The exact role of these genes in normal brain function will also become apparent. Specific features of ADHD will eventually be linked up to particular genes and medications to treat specific defects will be developed.

Male vulnerability to ADHD genes

ADHD is far more common in males that females. The explanation for this may lie in the well-documented differences between the frontal lobes of males and females.

All humans have two frontal lobes, a right and a left. These two lobes are structurally very different in males. For example, the outer layer (cortex) of the right frontal lobe is thicker than the left and has fewer dopamine pathways. In females, by contrast, the differences between the two lobes are not at all marked.

In ADHD a reversal of normal differences between the right and left frontal lobes occurs. It is believed that this is due to a compensating process. The use of alternative pathways to compensate for a defect in a particular area of the brain is well described in other brain disorders.

Females may be more capable of this type of compensating mechanism because their two frontal lobes are structurally and functionally so similar that transfer and sharing of functions between the two lobes can readily occur. In males, the structural differences between the two frontal lobes may make such transfers and sharing of functions less feasible.

This may explain why in males a relatively smaller number of ADHD genes may be sufficient to overwhelm their more limited compensatory mechanisms and cause ADHD, while females with the same number of genes may experience no signs of ADHD. It may also explain why many females seem to 'carry' the genes: they have a son who has the condition while not showing any signs of ADHD themselves.

Patterns of inheritance

If parents have had a child with ADHD, the chance of each successive child having ADHD is 5–6 times greater than for the general population, i.e., the risk increases to 1 in 3.

ADHD is a polygenic disorder requiring several genes acting in combination. This makes the pattern of inheritance of the condition complex and variable.

Often one of the parents of a child with ADHD also has the condition. In this situation the affected parent's genes are transmitted to the child and the inheritance is easy to understand.

The situation is more puzzling to parents when there is no history of ADHD in the family. In such a situation, it is probable that both parents carry a small number of ADHD genes that are insufficient to cause ADHD in them. It should be remembered that ADHD genes are common in the general population. When the genes from both parents combine in their child they may have an additive effect that is sufficient to cause the condition in the child.

Sometimes the presence of ADHD in a sibling of one or both of the parents indicates the presence of ADHD genes in the family. The affected sibling is often a brother of the mother of the child with ADHD. This occurs because a male is more vulnerable to ADHD genes as described above.

One of the results of so many different genes being involved in the causation of ADHD is that the condition does not always 'breed true' in a family. This means that ADHD may occur in different forms in different members of the same family. This is because the exact combination of ADHD genes that each affected sibling received from his or her parents may not be identical. In the same way, not all affected siblings in a family are necessarily helped by the same medicine.

Why co-morbidity occurs

Conditions that commonly co-exist with ADHD, the co-morbid disorders, are described in earlier chapters. These include tic disorder, dyslexia, oppositional disorder, conduct disorder, Asperger syndrome, depression, anxiety disorder, obsessive compulsive disorder, and bipolar disorder.

The co-morbid disorders that may co-exist with ADHD are also polygenetic in their causation. Co-morbidity occurs because ADHD and its associated conditions share some genes in common. Each co-morbid condition is caused by some ADHD genes together with additional genes unique to it. This is demonstrated for tic disorder in Figure 5.

Among the genes that cause ADHD are some that are involved in the causation of tics. A person with ADHD, therefore, only needs a few additional 'tic genes' in order to suffer tics as well as ADHD. As tic genes are common in the community, individuals with ADHD will often inherit the additional genes so that they have both ADHD and tics (co-morbidity). The same applies to all the other co-morbid conditions.

This explains some observed inter-relationships between different conditions that puzzled doctors in the past. For example, it was commonly observed that parents with bipolar disorder were more likely to have a child with ADHD and that such children were more likely to develop bipolar disorder later.

An explanation for this sequence of events is now possible. Some bipolar genes are also ADHD genes. These ADHD genes from the parents combine in the child and so are sufficient to cause ADHD. The ADHD in the child resolves at adolescence and at this time the bipolar disorder genes begin to express themselves for the first time.

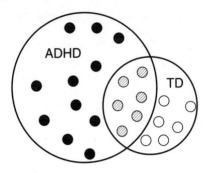

Figure 5 Co-morbidity and genes. ADHD and tic disorder (TD) share some of their genes.

This also explains why some of the characteristic features of ADHD are in fact milder forms of certain co-morbid emotional disorders. It may, for example, be the genes common to ADHD and depression that cause the dysthymia (low mood) that is often part of ADHD; similarly some of the obsessive-compulsive disorder genes that are common to ADHD may cause the preoccupations that often form part of ADHD. In this way the continuum of features can be explained: extending from a 'restless mind' to anxiety; from dysthymia to depression; and from preoccupations to obsessive-compulsive disorder. The severity of each will depend on the number of genes the person has inherited for that particular emotional disorder.

Frontal lobe changes during puberty

We are all familiar with the physical changes that occur in children's bodies at puberty. A 'genetic clock' that switches certain genes on at critical ages controls these changes.

The frontal lobes, too, are under the control of a genetic clock that allows them to become more competent as the child grows older. This is the very last part of the brain to mature, a process that occurs in the late teenage and early adult years. Much of the increase in self-control and self-direction (which we refer to as 'maturity') that occurs during late adolescence is due to dramatic changes in frontal lobe size and structure that occur at this stage of development.

As the frontal cortex matures, adolescents become more able to reason, they develop more control over their impulses, and their judgment improves. It is little wonder that the frontal lobes are referred to as the 'area of sober, second thought'.

The brain does not acquire any new brain cells after birth. For a part of the brain to start exerting a greater influence on behavior, nerve cells already present in that part of the brain must become more powerful and direct this power in an effective manner.

It is only recently, with the results of serial MRI scans (Magnetic Resonance Imaging) performed on normal children, that the mechanism behind these changes has become evident. The process occurs because the frontal lobes of adolescents undergo a stage of forming of new synapses ('synaptogenesis'). For the best outcome, such synapses must be precisely positioned to allow the individual to best meet the particular demands of his life. This is achieved by a second stage known as 'pruning'.

The first stage, synaptogenesis, occurs over the whole frontal lobes. It is a process unique to this part of the brain and is probably related to the initial surge in sex hormones levels early in puberty. Frontal lobe synaptogenesis peaks at the age of approximately 12 years of age.

In the second stage, newly formed synapses that are not used are discarded, a process known as 'pruning'. This is comparable to the pruning of a tree: weak branches are cut back while others are allowed to flourish. Frontal lobe pruning occurs in mid to late adolescence (between 13 and 18 years of age). During this period of pruning, an adolescent loses approximately 1% of his or her gray matter (nerve cells) every year.

The pruning stage is critical to the maturation of the frontal lobes. A synaptic 'power struggle' occurs: synapses that are used remain and exert their influence, those that are not used by the young adolescent are lost forever. This follows the 'use-it-or-lose-it' principle commonly observed in the study of the body. This process by which the frontal lobes are hard-wired (synapses permanently formed) is succinctly described by the rule: 'nerve cells that fire together, wire together'.

Frontal lobe synapses formed during late childhood and early adolescence are more likely to survive if the child is exercising his executive functions. The chance of a child growing out of his ADHD therefore improves if he is in an environment that encourages him to remain attentive, persist with tasks, and exercise self-control. It is also probable that children who take regular medication for ADHD are more likely to grow out of their condition than those who do not. This is because the medication encourages the child to use his executive functions more consistently and, as PET scans have demonstrated, ensures that frontal lobe nerve pathways are firing and transmitting impulses regularly throughout the frontal lobe network.

There is no doubt that many children with ADHD do show a remarkable improvement in their condition during late adolescence. The pruning process provides an opportunity for the frontal lobes to be 'rewired' in such a way as to compensate for the depleted levels of neurotransmitter.

Non-genetic factors

While ADHD is caused by genetic factors in the vast majority of cases, non-genetic conditions can play a causative role in some children with ADHD. They may be the primary cause or a contributing factor.

Any condition that causes sufficient damage to the frontal lobes can cause ADHD. Such conditions include severe head trauma, brain hemorrhage (which is more common in premature babies), lead poisoning (if it occurs before the age of 3 years), brain infection (meningitis or encephalitis), brain tumors, leukemia (particularly if treated with head radiotherapy), hydrocephalus, and neurofibromatosis.*

Some non-genetic causative factors will only give rise to ADHD in an individual who has a genetic susceptibility. In this situation the child has a small number of ADHD genes that are insufficient to cause ADHD on their own. The non-genetic condition acts as a contributing factor rather than as the primary cause of the ADHD. Such contributing factors include low birth weight, smoking during pregnancy, and alcohol abuse during pregnancy. In addition, any of the non-genetic causes listed in the previous paragraph could, if mild, act as a contributing factor rather than the primary cause.

The pediatrician who makes the diagnosis of ADHD in the child will be in the best position to assess whether any of these non-genetic factors played a role in causation.

*Neurofibromatosis is a genetic disorder, it is included with non-genetic disorders because the neurofibromatosis gene is not one of the ADHD genes.

Section 4

How ADHD is diagnosed

11

Diagnosis and assessment

The first step in the proper treatment of ADHD is making the diagnosis. Only when it is known that a child has ADHD and that all other possible causes of the problems have been excluded, can a proper treatment program be devised.

The best person to make the diagnosis is a specialist pediatrician with an interest and expertize in the area of developmental and learning difficulties in children. Such 'developmental pediatricians' work in close liaison with educational psychologists, who play a vital role in the process by which ADHD is diagnosed.

Diagnosis involves a number of steps. First, a careful history must be taken to collect information about how the child learns and behaves at home and at school. Often this will require that parents and the teachers fill out a standard questionnaire that has been designed to help make the diagnosis of ADHD.

Second, the pediatrician will carefully examine the child to ensure that there is no other condition interfering with her learning and/or behavior. He or she will arrange any further special investigations if necessary.

Third, special (psychometric) tests will need to be performed to develop an understanding of the child's particular areas of difficulty.

It is then the responsibility of the pediatrician to evaluate all this information and to make a diagnosis, which he or she should then explain to the parents.

The history

The pediatrician will ask questions in order to ascertain the child's special problems. He or she will want to know how long the parents have been concerned about the child, what concerns them, and which treatments have already been tried.

He or she will want to look at school reports to find out how the child is progressing and how teachers have evaluated the child over the years.

School reports are often written in an overly positive way because the teacher knows that the child will be reading the report and does not want to discourage her. It is therefore useful to ask the teacher to write a special letter for the pediatrician outlining the teacher's concerns about the child.

In some cases the teacher could be given a special checklist designed for children with ADHD in which he or she can tick off those symptoms that have been noted in the classroom.

Sometimes it is best if the teacher, with the parents' permission, rings the doctor to give a first-hand description of the child's behavior.

It is a good idea to obtain reports from other professionals who have seen the child in the past, and to show these to the pediatrician.

The pediatrician will also ask the parents about how their child behaves at home. It is best if both parents attend the assessment to enable both to give their views about the child. This will also allow both parents to hear the results and recommendations, and to have a say in any treatment plan that is developed.

The pediatrician will ask about the pregnancy and birth as well as about any health problems that the child has had. He or she will want to ensure that the child has adequate vision and hearing. It is a good idea to have both of these things checked before seeing the pediatrician. This should be done even if hearing and vision seem to be good in everyday situations, as minor difficulties are easily missed and may play a role in the child's learning problems. The family doctor will be able to arrange a referral to an ophthalmologist (a doctor specializing in eye disorders) and an audiologist (a technician trained to test hearing). If this cannot be organized before the consultation with the pediatrician, he or she may arrange for such testing to be done after the consultation.

The pediatrician will also enquire about any difficulties that may have been experienced by other family members. ADHD, as well as other learning difficulties, often runs in families and it is very useful in understanding the condition to know about other affected family members. It is a good idea for parents to ask their own parents about other family members before seeing the pediatrician.

The pediatrician may also give parents a questionnaire to fill in to obtain more detailed information about the child's behavior. These questionnaires are used as a guide and have been administered to many thousands of parents in order to obtain an idea of what constitutes normal behavior.

The examination

It is essential that the pediatrician carefully examines the child to ensure that the child does not have a condition other than ADHD that interferes with learning. He or she will check the child's growth (height, weight, and head size). He or she will search for any unusual features in the child's body that suggest one of the rare genetic syndromes that are associated with learning difficulties.

The pediatrician will examine the nervous system with particular care looking for any abnormality ('hard' neurological signs). This is done by checking the child's balance and coordination, as well as her muscular strength, muscular tone, and reflexes. The pediatrician will also test the functioning of various nerves in the body.

Developmental pediatricians also look for 'soft' neurological signs that are more subtle signs of immaturity in the way in which the brain processes sensations and controls movements. These signs do not have the same implications as hard neurological signs, but do indicate that the child is not yet functioning as maturely as other children of her age. Soft neurological signs are very common in children with ADHD.

There are a number of conditions that the pediatrician needs to exclude before a diagnosis of ADHD can be made. He or she needs to know that the child does not have a vision or hearing impairment that is causing the problem. Intellectual disability must be excluded. Physical disability, such as cerebral palsy, must also be excluded. Such conditions may be present in some children, but may not explain all the child's difficulties. They may act as an aggravating factor in a child whose primary problem is ADHD. For example, a child may have mild intellectual disability, but may have problems with concentration and impulsivity that are excessive for her degree of intellectual disability. Such a child may have ADHD as well as intellectual disability and may benefit from treatment of the ADHD.

Psychometric testing

Careful evaluation of a child's particular areas of strength and weakness is essential in order to make the correct diagnosis, as well as to plan appropriate strategies for helping the child. It is only by this sort of evaluation that certain conditions that mimic ADHD, such as intellectual disability, can be excluded.

Once the child's particular areas of strength and weakness are established, an individualized treatment program can be planned. For example, a child with ADHD who has reading problems will need a different sort of help from the child with ADHD who is a proficient reader.

The evaluation of a child's particular areas of strength and weakness requires individualized testing by an experienced educational psychologist using a battery of standardized 'psychometric' tests. The tests that are generally used have been administered to many hundreds of children to obtain standards for different ages. They have been carefully devised to compare an individual child's skills to those of his or her contemporaries. In this way one can determine whether a child is advanced, delayed, or age appropriate in different areas of development.

Tasks are presented in a specific order with the easier ones first. They then become progressively more advanced to establish at what level they become too difficult for the child. Every child who does the test will be presented with tasks that are easy, as well as tasks that are too difficult for her. This is necessary in order to find out the exact level at which she is functioning.

During the course of the test, a picture of the child's developmental progress can be formed, both for specific areas of development and for development as a whole. Sometimes a great deal of information can be gained from the way in which the child tackles tasks, even if she is unable to succeed. For example, the psychologist will observe her ability to persist with tasks, to attend for long periods, and to sit still.

The psychologist will choose tests that are most useful for the particular child. There are now many tests available and the psychologist will usually select a number of these. Children with suspected ADHD should be given a test of intelligence, tests of academic achievement, and certain other tests of special ability.

Tests of intelligence

Although intelligence tests have come in for criticism over the past few years, they still form an essential part of establishing a child's abilities and needs. They must be performed by an experienced educational psychologist, and interpreted with care. The results of the tests should be regarded as only part of the child's assessment and need to be interpreted in the light of reports of his or her abilities at other times and the results of any previous tests.

Intelligence tests assess general intelligence. Many are very well suited to children with learning difficulties because they do not involve any reading or writing. They can, therefore, test intelligence irrespective of academic achievement. Intelligence tests not only establish the child's level of general intelligence, but also give valuable information about individual components of intelligence, such as short-term memory and sequential processing.

The different tasks in the most widely used intelligence tests are usually grouped into a number of 'sub-tests'; the score of each sub-test reflects a particular area of intelligence. The sub-tests for one of the most common intelligence tests for school age children, the Wechsler Intelligence Scale for Children—third edition (WISC-III) are grouped together to give a *verbal score*, which is a measure of the child's ability in language-related tasks, and a *performance score*, which is related to visual and manual tasks. A comparison of these scores will show if a child is having particular difficulties in one of these areas.

Another useful score which can be obtained from the WISC-III is known as the *freedom from distractability index* which refers to the child's performance on those parts of the test that require persistence with tedious tasks. Many, but not all, children with ADHD score poorly in this area.

Another part of the WISC-III where children with ADHD often score poorly is the 'digits backwards' part of the Digit Span sub-test. Whereas the 'digits forward' part requires only a good rote memory, digits backwards requires a competent working memory, a weak area in these children.

In interpreting these various components of intelligence tests, it is important to keep in mind the child's overall level of skill. For example, a highly intelligent child who is functioning in the 'superior' range may be regarded as having difficulties in concentration if her score in the *freedom from distractability index* is only in the 'average' range. On the other hand, such a score in the *freedom from distractability index* would be considered acceptable in a child whose overall intellectual function was also in the 'average' range.

Tests of academic achievement

These include tests of reading, spelling, and mathematics. It is essential that all children with ADHD have these tests in addition to an intelligence test. It is not uncommon for a child who is thought to be functioning adequately at school to be found to have an unrecognized difficulty in one or more aspects of academic competence.

Academic achievement tests establish the level of a child's skills in a particular area of learning compared to her peers and also give important information about the nature of a child's difficulties in the area tested. The results will be given in terms of an age equivalency, i.e. the age at which the average child is able to function in the same way as the child who was tested. Some test results are expressed in 'percentiles', which indicate the percentage of children who would function less well at the same age. For example, a child with spelling competence on the 45th percentile would be functioning better than 44% of children of the same age (and less well than 55% of children of the same age).

These tests compare children to others of the same age. Allowance may be necessary for children who started school at a later age than usual. Having been at school for a shorter period of time than most children of their age, it should be anticipated that their academic attainments would reflect this, rather than any lack of potential on the child's part.

Reading tests

Because the written word constitutes one of the most important ways in which children learn, reading is one of the most vital skills for children to acquire. The child with slow or inaccurate reading, and/or difficulties with reading comprehension, is at a great disadvantage. Reading difficulties are common in children with ADHD.

There are a number of reading tests available to psychologists. Usually the child will be asked to read aloud from portions of text that have been graded according to difficulty. These texts have few, simple words in large print, often with illustrations. The child will progress to more and more difficult levels until it is clear to the tester that the child has reached her limit.

The tests usually determine the child's reading speed relative to other children of her age. The number of errors the child makes is also noted to establish reading accuracy, which is compared to age standards. After each portion of text is read, the tester may ask the child a number of standardized questions about what she has just read to determine the child's reading comprehension. This, too, can be compared to age standards.

Reading speed, accuracy, and comprehension can all be expressed in age levels. For example, a child of 9 years and 2 months may have a reading accuracy at a 6 year 3 month level, if she makes the same number of mistakes as the average 6 year 3 month old; she will have a reading comprehension age of 6 years 5 months, if she understands what she has read as well as an average 6 year 5 month old.

In addition to these scores, the tester is interested in the particular types of errors the child makes. He or she may also give the child some specific tests to try to establish the exact nature of the reading problem. For example, he or she may test the child's visual perception: the brain's ability to make sense of what is seen. He or she may compare the child's ability to read real and nonsense words to evaluate her phonological (sounding out) skills.

Many children with ADHD will be found to have difficulties with reading speed, accuracy, and reading comprehension. In such children, it is important to distinguish those who have difficulties with reading comprehension *per se* and those whose reading comprehension simply reflects the fact that they are inaccurate readers. Some children may be able to understand something that is read fluently to them, but have difficulty extracting the meaning of something they read themselves. This does not indicate any difficulty with verbal comprehension, but simply difficulties with the process of reading itself. The remedial help for such a child would need to concentrate on reading accuracy. Reading comprehension would then improve. Other children may have difficulties understanding language and will need help in verbal comprehension. This requires the involvement of a speech therapist.

There are many children who find it embarrassing to read out aloud. For such children, a reading test that requires reading a passage to the psychologist may under-estimate their true reading accuracy and comprehension. It is impossible to measure reading accuracy without having the child read aloud, but it may be helpful to have the child read a passage silently to herself before asking questions that determine her reading comprehension. There are tests for measuring silent reading comprehension.

Spelling tests

Spelling is another important area that should be assessed. There are several standardized spelling tests in general use. These differ in the way in which they test spelling. Some present the child with words that are part of her sight vocabulary, others present a wider range of words.

Tests usually involve spelling from dictation. Some may also involve recognizing whether a printed word is correctly spelt or not.

The psychologist will choose the test or tests that provide information about the child's spelling level, as well as about the nature of her difficulties. For example, a test that shows that a child has difficulties with spelling from dictation, but not with identifying words that are incorrectly spelt, may demonstrate particular problems with auditory discrimination (distinguishing sounds) or word memory.

The psychologist will also try to differentiate between different kinds of spelling errors, such as phonetic (words that look right but sound wrong), visual (words that sound right but look wrong), and sequential (for example 'brigde' for 'bridge') errors.

Arithmetic tests

The assessment of arithmetic skills becomes more difficult as children reach higher levels of proficiency in mathematics. For younger children, or children with significant difficulties in arithmetic, the psychologist may obtain sufficient information about the child's arithmetical ability from the *Arithmetic* sub-test of the WISC-III. This test does not require the child to write down the answers. The problems are timed and relate to various arithmetical skills.

Addition, subtraction, multiplication, and division can all be tested. Some problems also require memorized number facts and subtle operations, such as seeing relevant relationships at a glance. The emphasis of the test is not on mathematical knowledge as such, but on mental computations and concentration.

The WISC-III will also give the psychologist information about other abilities that relate to arithmetical processes. In the *Digit span* sub-test, the child's ability to remember numbers for a short period is tested. As stated earlier in this chapter, the digits backwards part of this test is a measure of working memory, an essential part of carrying out arithmetical operations in the brain. For example, in order to add 2 to 3, the 2 must be held in the working memory while 3 is added to it. Children with ADHD often have low scores in the digits backward part of the Digit span sub-test. This may relate partly to difficulties with working memory and partly to difficulties with auditory attention span.

In the *Comprehension* sub-test, verbal reasoning is involved. If, for example, a child has high comprehension but low arithmetic scores, this may suggest that reasoning ability is adequate in social situations, but not in situations involving numbers.

If the psychologist wants further information on arithmetical ability, there are a number of tests that specifically test mathematical skills and enable the results to be compared with those of children of the same age. They may also allow the psychologist to diagnose the precise difficulty that is interfering with the child's arithmetical performance. This will allow the remedial teacher to devise methods of providing specific help in the area of difficulty.

Tests of other special abilities

Children with suspected ADHD should have careful assessment of their auditory and visual attention span, using standardized tests for skills such as vigilance (ability to allocate attention to a new stimulus), task persistence, distractability, and short-term (working) memory.

These tests may be computerized. For example, in one commonly used test of vigilance, the child has to push a button whenever a particular number sequence (the stimulus) appears on the computer screen. The computer analyses the child's performance and compares it to standards for her age.

Such tests play an important part in helping the developmental pediatrician to make the diagnosis of ADHD. They cannot be used in isolation, but form part of the information that is required to determine whether the child has ADHD or not. They may also play an important role in determining the child's response to treatment and in reviewing the child's progress over time.

Many children with ADHD have difficulties with handwriting and written expression. Children with ADHD often have difficulties with written expression. They find it very difficult to write about a topic. Children commonly say that the writing 'won't come'. It is impossible to score a sample of writing in a precise way. Samples of writing are usually evaluated by an experienced tester. Three samples of writing are obtained: a passage of free composition on a particular topic, a piece of dictation, and a copy of some printed material. In the case of the free composition, the child is usually given a limited amount of time, such as five minutes. In the other two tests, she is timed to see how long she takes. In this way, the tester can see how quickly the child writes, as well as assess the legibility of the samples and study them to determine the nature of the child's difficulty. He or she will also observe the child's posture and method of holding the pen or pencil.

In addition to the writing test, the psychologist may do other tests, such as tests of drawing and visual perception.

Children with difficulties with handwriting or with other fine motor skills, such as drawing, using scissors, or tying knots, should have standardized tests performed by an occupational therapist. Children with gross motor difficulty, in such activities as walking, running, jumping, hopping, or bicycle riding, may need to be referred by the developmental pediatrician to a physiotherapist for standardized testing.

Children with ADHD often have difficulties with language. These may affect receptive language (understanding), expressive language (the ability to put words together), or speech (the clarity of the spoken word). A child with suspected language difficulties should be assessed by a speech therapist (sometimes called a speech pathologist). Such an assessment involves both informal observation and standardized tests to evaluate speech, expressive language, and receptive language. In addition to establishing the child's level of development in these areas, the speech therapist will determine the specific nature of her difficulties. No such testing should be performed until the child's hearing has also been properly tested.

Special investigations

If the pediatrician considers it necessary, he or she will arrange special investigations to determine the cause of the child's difficulties. These investigations include blood tests and brain scans. Such testing is not done routinely.

If a child who has poor concentration seems to have 'blank' episodes, the pediatrician may arrange for a special brain wave test called an EEG (electroencephalogram) to be performed in order to determine if the child is having a type of epilepsy that causes very short 'blank spells'. Occasionally this condition may be mistaken for the inattentive type of ADHD. A special fabric cap is placed on the child's head. The cap has wires that are connected to a computer. The computer measures the child's brainwaves and prints them on paper.

An ordinary EEG cannot determine if a child has ADHD; however, there are some special tests of brain electricity that have been used to obtain objective measures of brain activity that are more useful in diagnosing ADHD.

For such testing a far more sophisticated analysis of the brain electricity is performed. As in the case of an ordinary EEG test, an injection is not required, radiation is not involved, and there is no discomfort to the child. It is completely safe. The analysis of the brain waves is performed while the child carries out three tasks: concentrating on a special pattern produced on a screen, counting intermittent tones produced through headphones, and sitting still with the eyes closed. The results of this testing gives rise to a scan of the brain known as a QEEG and a composite of brain wave patterns known as a cognitive event-related potential.

QEEG

Computerized quantitative analysis of EEG signals (QEEG) allows brain activity to be compared to that of a normal child of the same age, using stored data. This can be represented in a colored picture.

A QEEG of a normal child is compared to a characteristic QEEG seen in ADHD in Figure 6. In the child with ADHD, the electricity measured over the frontal part of the brain shows excess slow (theta) wave activity. This is normal activity that originates from structures at the base of the brain. It is not detected in large amounts over the surface of the brain because faster frontal lobe activity screens it out. Children with ADHD characteristically have decreased activity in the frontal part of the brain and so this screening out does not occur. Figure 3 demonstrates that these slow waves disappear when frontal lobe activity increases after medication for ADHD is taken.

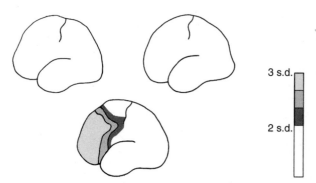

Figure 6 QEEGs: normal (above left), ADHD before treatment (below), ADHD after treatment (above right). The shaded area shows excess theta activity for age [s.d. = standard deviations, a measure of difference from normal].

Cognitive event-related potentials

The second type of information obtained from specialized analysis of brainwaves relates to what is known as 'a cognitive event-related potential' (ERP).

A cognitive event-related potential measures changes in the electrical activity of the brain that occur when specific tasks are undertaken. For example, when asked to listen for a sound, a child must allocate attention, and an event-related potential recorded when the child attends to the sound will contain elements that reflect the deployment of attentional capacity that takes place in the brain.

When children with ADHD concentrate intently on a sound, they do not generate the strong waves on cognitive event-related potentials that normal children do. In children with ADHD, certain waves on cognitive event-related potentials are smaller and occur later.

Figure 7 shows the cognitive event-related potential of a normal child who counted tones heard infrequently. A wave, known as the P300, indicates that the attentional mechanism is working efficiently.

Figure 8(a) shows the cognitive event-related potential of a child with ADHD carrying out the same task. This child, too, counted the correct number of tones, but it is clear that the P300 is not properly formed.

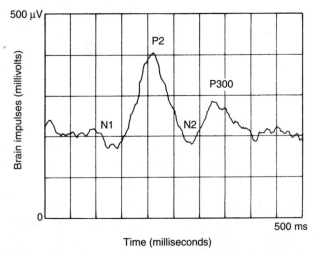

Figure 7 A normal cognitive event-related potential.

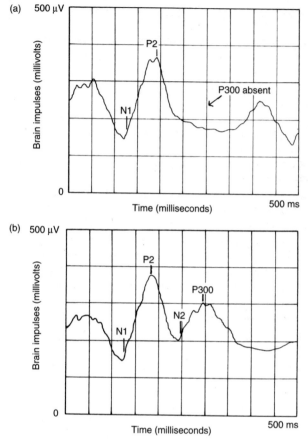

Figure 8 Cognitive event-related potentials: (a) ADHD before treatment; (b) ADHD after treatment.

It can be inferred that the child has to concentrate using a less efficient attentional mechanism. Figure 8(b) shows how the size of the P300 improves when the child is taking medicine for ADHD.

The role of the QEEG and cognitive event-related potentials

QEEG and cognitive event-related potential testing provide objective evidence of the brain inefficiencies that cause ADHD. They cannot be used in isolation, but may form *part* of the information that is required to determine whether the child has ADHD or not. They are not yet widely available and many children are treated without access to this kind of evaluation.

Formulation of a management plan

Once the developmental pediatrician has collected together information about the child, a treatment plan can be developed. The pediatrician will provide a thorough explanation of the findings shortly after the examination. He or she will also make recommendations about ways of helping the child.

Parents should remember that these are only suggestions; they know their child and family best, and will need to decide whether they feel that the recommendations are right for their child and their family. If they feel unhappy with any of the suggestions, they should not hesitate to tell the pediatrician so that alternative strategies can be found.

Each treatment plan will be tailored to the child's particular areas of difficulty. There is no single approach that suits all children. Children with difficulties in a particular academic area may need remedial help, while others who are proficient in the area will not.

Medication should be considered for all children with significant difficulties, but this decision, too, needs to be individualized.

Review assessments

If a child's problems resolve, reassessment will not be needed; however, if the child continues to have difficulties, further assessments should be carried out to monitor the child's progress and ensure that any special needs are met.

Reviews usually occur every 6 months and involve physical examination, psychometric testing, and any other special testing to determine how the child is progressing. A report from the child's teacher should be requested for all reviews.

Section 5

Multi-model treatment

12
Home management

Children with ADHD are very challenging to bring up. No parent of a child with ADHD will be able to respond to every difficulty that arises in a textbook manner. Children with ADHD often bring out the worst in their parents, and even the most patient and understanding parent is likely to make many mistakes.

All that a parent of a child with ADHD should hope to achieve is to be a 'good enough' parent—a parent who tries to do his or her best, who learns from his or her mistakes, and who provides support for the child through all the difficulties that life presents.

Understanding—the first step in management

No plan of management can ever be successful if it is not based on a comprehensive assessment of the child's particular strengths and difficulties, as described in the previous chapter, and a careful explanation to both the parents, and the child, of the nature of the condition.

Unfortunately, there is a great tendency to blame any behavioral or learning difficulty on inadequacy on the part of the parents or an intentional failure on the part of the child. This belief is deeply rooted in the way in which we interpret children's behavior. Understanding ADHD requires a shift in our way of thinking about and perceiving children's actions.

We are almost unable to think of the brain as an organ, just like the lungs or the heart, and to realize that its primary function is to control behavior and learning. All behavior is controlled by the brain.

One often hears comments such as 'His poor concentration is not due to ADHD, it is behavioral!'. However, to say that a behavior is or is not 'behavioral' is in reality meaningless. A behavior has to be 'behavioral'—that is what that adjective means. What the person probably means by the word 'behavioral' is that the behavior is in some way due to inadequate child rearing, or some vague notion of 'naughtiness' on the part of the child. That the word 'behavioral' has become almost synonymous with such causation tells us a great deal about how lopsided our view of the causes of children's behavior has become.

There is no doubt that a child can behave in an unwanted way because of poor child-rearing experiences, but this is not the only, or necessarily the most common, cause of behavioral difficulties.

All unwanted behaviors in children should be looked at objectively to determine causation. Some will be due to an inadequacy in the way in which the child has been reared, many will be due to an inefficiency in the child's brain, and some will be due to a mixture of the two. In other cases the cause may best be viewed as a mismatch between the child's brain and the environmental demands that are placed on him.

It is interesting that when children have difficulty walking we point to their legs as the likely cause of the problem; if they have difficulty breathing, we point to their lungs; when they have difficulty hearing we point to their ears—but when they have difficulty behaving, we point to their parents!

Only a careful assessment can tease out the factors that relate to child rearing and those that relate to immaturities in the child's brain. Then a proper understanding and management plan can be devised.

Once it is determined that the child's difficulties are due to ADHD, we must look upon the child as someone whose behavior and learning inadequacies are due to a hidden disability that is not of his, or his parents', making. Once this is understood, the child can be helped.

Explaining to the child

Parents are sometimes concerned about telling their child that he has ADHD in case he becomes upset about knowing that there is an inefficiency in his brain. However, children with ADHD know from an early age that there is something different about them. They know that they are getting into more trouble than other children or that they are struggling to learn things that other children are learning with ease.

Children start to compare themselves with their peers from a very early age and are quick to notice which things they find difficult. Unfortunately, if parents or professionals do not explain to the child with ADHD the cause of his problems, the child is likely to come to the conclusion that he is 'dumb' or 'stupid'. Children with ADHD have a tendency to find a locus of blame for things that go wrong in their lives, as described in Chapter 7, and therefore can easily become angry and depressed by their difficulties.

It is therefore a good idea to tell your child about ADHD at an early stage. Do not wait until he becomes confused and discouraged. Explain that different people are talented in different ways. Point out those things at which he is better, and the special qualities he has. Tell him about the things that you find difficult. Then explain that some things are very difficult for him to do, even when he tries very hard. Explain that this is simply because a part of his brain is taking a little longer to switch itself on completely.

Explain that as children grow, changes occur in their bodies. They get new teeth, they grow taller, they become stronger, their bodies change into those of adults, etc. Explain that there is a little mechanism in the brain that is very important for helping a person to concentrate and control frustration and that this becomes stronger as children grow older. Describe it as being like a switch that is slowly turned on.

Just as some children get their teeth a little later, or go into puberty a little later, so in children with ADHD this 'switch' takes longer to turn on completely.

Emphasize that the switch is already partly on and that the child can already concentrate and control his behavior, but that it is far more difficult for him to do these things. You may need to explain that that is why he sometimes finds it difficult to sustain his attention, control his impulsivity, or manage to win friends.

It is important that children with ADHD realize that they can do the things they find difficult, and that they are not led to believe that these things are impossible for them to achieve. However, it is essential to acknowledge the great difficulty that they experience in trying to be consistent in performing certain tasks.

There are now many good books that are written for children with ADHD to explain their condition to them. These include two books written by Dr Michael Gordon: 'Jumpin Johnny Get Back To Work!' for the younger child, and 'I Would If I Could' for the teenager. Jeanne Gehret has also written an excellent book for children, 'Eagle Eyes—A Child's View of Attention Deficit Disorder'. Other good books include: 'Shelley, The Hyperactive Turtle' (age 3–7) by Deborah Moss;

'The "Putting On The Brakes" Activity Book For Young People with ADD', by Patricia Quinn and Judith Stern; and two books by Roberta Parker: 'Making The Grade' and 'Slam Dunk' which are both suitable for adolescents.

For younger children who need to take medicine for ADHD, 'Otto Learns About His Medicine' explains medical treatment of ADHD through a story.

All books and videos recommended here can be ordered from ADD WareHouse (see Appendix for website).

Parents' needs

Before looking at ways of helping your child, it is essential to look at your own needs and concerns. Parents need help in coping with their own feelings and those of their other children, as well as other members of the family.

It is quite natural to feel guilty about your child's difficulties. Most parents report that they imagine that they are in some way to blame for the fact that their child has ADHD. This may be aggravated when they find out that ADHD has a very strong genetic aspect to its causation and that it tends to run in families. You need to understand that ADHD is due to constitutional factors within your child and is not due to anything that is under your control. Every person carries a wide variety of genes and no one can be held responsible for his or her genetic make-up. Genes, good and bad, are passed from generation to generation in a way that is beyond our control. ADHD genes are very common in the community and ADHD is usually due to a combination of genes from both parents.

Because ADHD runs in families, parents have often had similar difficulties to their child and this can be a double-edged sword. On the one hand, having experienced similar difficulties gives you more insight into the problems your child has faced, or may face, in the future. On the other hand, you are likely to strongly identify with your child and may find that this makes it more difficult to cope with the fact that he may go through the same problems, and suffer the same hurt, that you experienced.

If you have the residual form of ADHD that persists into adulthood, you will need to be aware that your own difficulties with impulsivity and rigidity might make it more difficult for you to help your child. If this is the case, you may need professional guidance to help you manage. However, parents who have had ADHD do have an advantage in that they usually understand their children's difficulties in a way that other parents cannot.

Parents of children with ADHD experience many emotions. They may be hurt by other people's insensitive remarks about their child, they may be embarrassed by their child's difficulties, and they may feel great anxiety about how their child will cope both academically and socially. Many parents feel overwhelmed by the task of teaching their child to overcome his difficulties. They may feel angry much of the time, too—angry with teachers who fail to understand their child's problems and angry with doctors who fail to recognize their child's difficulties.

Despite these difficulties, most parents do cope and find that things become easier with time. It may be helpful to have someone with whom to share your feelings: a friend, a spouse, or professional, someone who will listen sympathetically and not be judgmental or too quick to offer advice.

It can be very helpful to meet other parents of a child with similar difficulties. There are now many support groups for parents of children with ADHD and some of these may be obtained from the websites listed in the Appendix of this book. Support groups invite speakers who help broaden and deepen your understanding of your child's difficulties. They will also assist with strategies to manage your child.

Support groups often produce a newsletter and may have a lending library of books and videos. The greatest strength of such groups is that they allow parents to meet informally and exchange experiences.

When a professional or other parent provides advice, you should always feel free to reject this if it does not fit in with your own child-rearing practices, or your own family's way of doing things. There is no one single right way of helping children with ADHD, or of coping with the difficulties that you face. There is no single prescription that will work for everyone. Choose those things that seem right to you and fit in best with your way of doing things.

One of the most important things is to try to take one step at a time. Set yourself realistic short-term goals and concentrate on them. Try to avoid looking too far ahead. After all, your child, you, and the opportunities available to you will change in ways that cannot always be predicted.

Children with ADHD cause their parents a lot of stress. It is important to find ways of reducing your own stress levels. Some parents will attend relaxation classes or stress management courses. Whenever possible, find ways of recharging your own batteries. Difficulties can often be solved when you have a chance to stand back and see things in perspective.

You may also need to develop strategies for coping with other people's hurtful remarks about your child. It is worthwhile giving some thought to this so that you do not find yourself unprepared.

First, you can set an example. If someone says something inappropriate, you can simply repeat what they have said in a more appropriate way. Some parents are helped by giving themselves silent pep talks, such as 'this man doesn't know what he is talking about'.

If you know that you are going to experience a difficult but unavoidable situation, it may be worth while rehearsing the situation before it takes place. You may do this on your own or with someone close to you. You will probably decide on a series of responses that are more appropriate than those that would have occurred without rehearsal. Sometimes such responses can be used on subsequent occasions in similar situations.

It is also important to provide information to those around you so that they understand your child's difficulties. It may be helpful to lend a book, such as this one, to a friend who does not understand your child's condition.

The needs of brothers and sisters

Siblings of a child with ADHD experience special pressures. It is important that they understand the nature of ADHD, that they receive attention of their own from parents, and that they develop strategies to help cope with the attitudes and comments of other children toward their brother or sister who has ADHD.

You should explain to the siblings that the child with ADHD is not lazy or naughty but that he has genuine difficulties in certain areas. Explain how you are trying to help him. It is important that you explain to the siblings that each child is different and that is why you have different expectations and different rules and regulations for each child. If this is explained carefully and carried out consistently, children can understand that they are not being discriminated against when it is necessary to spend more time with, or to show greater leniency toward, the child with ADHD.

It is important to distinguish between disability and laziness. A child with ADHD should not be able to use his disability as an excuse for quitting when a goal is attainable.

If a sibling is being teased about his brother or sister, it is important to acknowledge how hurt he must feel. Encourage him to express his anger and resentment and respond sympathetically. It is often difficult for a sibling to ignore unkind comments from his peers. It may help your child to imagine that he has an 'electric forcefield' surrounding his body that deflects any insults before they get to him.

It may be beneficial to ask the teacher to provide some help too. Sometimes a teacher can initiate a discussion about 'being different', or 'having difficulties' that may change the attitudes of other children.

The sibling of a child with ADHD may also benefit from the books written for children with ADHD and also some excellent videos, such as '*It's Just Attention Disorder: A video for kids*', that will give him or her insight into the difficulties a child with ADHD experiences. Two excellent books for siblings are '*I'm Somebody Too*' by Jean Geheret and '*My Brother's A World Class Pain*'.

Improving your child's self-esteem

Children with ADHD are often very hard on themselves. They appraise themselves harshly and are quick to blame themselves for things that go wrong. As explained in Chapter 7, this is partly related to immaturities in certain parts of the brain. In addition, children with ADHD are often failing academically and socially. It is therefore very important that parents help children build up their self-esteem as much as possible. This is important as many of the unwanted behaviors seen in children with ADHD, such as school avoidance, homework avoidance, TV addiction, cheating, aggression, controlling behavior, bullying, quitting and depression, are maladaptive responses to low self-esteem.

The most detrimental effect of low self-esteem is that it encourages a child to enter a cycle of failure in which his ability drops lower and lower. The child tries to evade failure by avoiding challenges. This results in poor attainments that reinforce the child's feeling of inadequacy. By contrast, a child with better self-esteem will be able to try harder because he is not so frightened of failure. Because children with ADHD appraise themselves so harshly, parents need to try to boost their child's self-esteem.

Many a parent of a child with ADHD has praised their child in the hope that this would bolster his or her self-image, only to find that the child reacted adversely to praise. The reason is that, because the child feels so inadequate, the praise reminds him of how poor his achievements are. Children with low self-esteem are often quick to misinterpret parental praise as being patronizing. Some children with ADHD are so insecure that they interpret praise as implied criticism or suspect that they are being compared with another child.

Yet parents need to develop their child's self-esteem. If a child with ADHD has not attained good self-esteem by adulthood, he will derive little value from any other success that he attains. With high self-esteem, he will probably cope well with life, even though some difficulties persist.

How can you as parents engender high self-esteem in your child with ADHD? First, you should accept your child for what he is; that is, the sum total of his strengths and weaknesses. You need to see him in terms of his own uniqueness. Try to see within him the potential that he will realize at his own pace.

As parents, your role is to encourage, enjoy and value him. Try to avoid basing your own feelings of self-esteem and worth on your child's behavior. Your child needs love that is not conditional upon his achievement. You also need to accept his feelings without criticism.

Try to emphasize his positive attributes and show how you value them. He needs plenty of praise for his efforts. However, do not overdo this or persist with praise if it clearly makes him feel uncomfortable. When praising, make it clear what you are praising him for. Avoid general comments such as, 'Well done', or 'Good boy', but rather say things such as, 'You spelt that difficult word very well', or, 'That was excellent reading'. Praise effort and not just achievement. However, when you praise effort, make it clear that it is effort you are praising. The child who tries very hard, but reads hesitantly, should be praised not for 'reading well', but for 'having a very good go'.

Children learn self-esteem from their parents' example. This is one of the reasons that children whose parents have high self-esteem are more likely to have high self-esteem themselves. You need to have faith in yourself. Let your child hear you praise your own accomplishments ('that was a job well done').

It is most important that you encourage your child to set realistic goals so that he can experience success. Help him to evaluate his achievements realistically so that he is not over-critical of himself.

It is important to set achievable goals at the start of any activity. If your child is going to attempt something that is too difficult for him, guide him to a more suitable activity in a tactful way.

You should also teach your child to praise himself. If he achieves something, ask him 'How do you think you went?' Teach him also to praise others (for example, 'what do you think of Dad's salad?').

Children benefit from having special time with both parents. Often one parent will have little opportunity for special time. This may be because he or she is so busy with home duties and chores, or with work outside the home, that he or she never has special time with the child. Both parents should plan ways in which children will have some special time with both of them. Special time does not necessarily mean that you have to organize activities away from home. It is time when you are able to give your attention to your child in a way that builds up his self-esteem. The important thing is that it should be enjoyable for the child and that he should be receiving your full attention.

Where parents are separated, children will have better self-esteem if they are not treated as a 'football' to be fought over by the parents. Parents owe it to their children to ensure that they work out peaceful and stable access arrangements even if this means some compromise on the part of one of the parents.

Children also need to feel that they belong to something. It may be an idea to arrange for your child to join a hobby group, a scout pack, or some other such unit. Encourage him to be proud of his school, his neighborhood, and his ethnic tradition.

Children need to feel that they have the power to make some of the choices that affect their lives. Whenever possible, let your child select things for himself, such as which clothes he wears, in what order he does things, and which books he takes from the library. Admire his choices and praise his self-sufficiency.

Another way of increasing your child's self-esteem is by enriching his experiences. Take him on excursions, teach him to do new things like gardening. Make a photo album with pictures of him. Give him opportunities to become self-reliant. Teach him to make small purchases on his own, to answer the telephone, and to take responsibility for some household task.

Your role as a teacher

Parents have an important role in helping their child to learn. They teach by example, often without realising it, and in a more direct way. For a child with ADHD, the parents' role as teacher becomes even more important. No other teacher can spend as much one-to-one time with a child. No other teacher has the opportunity to extend what the child has learned in so many different situations. However, a child's relationship with his parents is generally so much more intense than with any other teacher that parents should approach teaching with care. Most parents can be good at teaching their child provided they make this a positive and constructive experience for the child. This means that the parent must be prepared to put some thought into how to become an effective teacher.

Before you teach your child, you should liaise with his class teacher. He or she will ensure that what you teach complements what is being done at school. A good teacher will be happy to give you guidance about what to teach and how to go about it. He or she will be only too aware that there is usually insufficient time to give adequate individual tuition to each child in the class.

When you teach your child, do not overdo it. Short daily sessions are much better than infrequent long sessions. Attempt small units of work at a time. Do ensure that you are teaching your child the things that he is learning at school. You do not want to add to his burden by increasing the amount he has to learn. Aim to make those things that he already has to do at school easier.

Choose a time when you are both feeling calm. You need a quiet environment where you will not be disturbed. It may be necessary for you to arrange for your other children to be occupied somewhere else. Do not have a teaching session when you are doing something else, while the TV is on, or when siblings are around.

Try to make sessions as enjoyable and as varied as possible. Start with a revision of the previous work, and explain what you hope to achieve in this session and why it is important. Work slowly and patiently. Sometimes your child will seem to have a block or forget things that he knew the previous day. Take this in your stride. It is perfectly normal for children to progress slowly, with sudden spurts followed by protracted periods of comparatively little progress. During these slow phases children are often consolidating skills before going on to the next stage.

Because children with ADHD have to work so hard to concentrate, you may need to have frequent breaks. Some children benefit from having a chance to burn off excess energy before they start work. Other children will become so excited by physical activity that they then find it difficult to settle down to do homework afterwards. Children with ADHD who have difficulty in focusing after intense physical activity may be better working first and engaging in physical activities later.

The timing of the child's medication is very important with regard to when it is best to do homework or study. For example, a child who takes dexamphetamine or Ritalin (methylphenidate) in the afternoon should probably start working approximately one hour after the tablet has been taken. In this way he will be most settled when needed.

When working with your child, always be encouraging, never critical. Avoid expressions such as 'Hurry up', 'Watch what you're doing', 'Don't be careless', and 'You have seen that word before'. Instead, use phrases such as 'You are really improving at reading', and 'You really worked hard on this'.

Whenever you have a teaching session with your child, end it with an activity that he is good at and enjoys. At the end, do not forget to say something like 'That was fun, I look forward to doing some more with you tomorrow'. When the session is over, try to stop playing the part of the teacher. You are more than a teacher, you are a parent as well. Parents cannot treat every interaction with their child as an opportunity for teaching without the relationship becoming stilted and the child becoming resentful. There must be opportunities for unstructured interaction.

Teaching has to concentrate on the child's areas of weakness. Most children are aware from an early age of things they find difficult. Like the rest of us, they want to spend time on the things they are better at. Make certain that you give your child ample opportunities to do those things that he is good at, in addition to those he finds difficult. This is essential for his self-confidence.

Some parents do not have the time or the ability to teach their child. In this case, it is usually best to find a teacher or coach to help your child after school. It is important to choose someone with the skills and temperament to do this well. Support organizations often have lists of suitable teachers. The names of some of these organizations can be found via the websites whose addresses are listed in the Appendix.

Working with the school

It is best to regard yourself, the teachers, and other professionals (such as speech therapists) involved with your child's education as a team. Each member of the team plays a part in providing the best education for the child. It is essential that you and the other members of the team communicate regularly.

Some schools have a file for each child that is passed on to his new teacher every year. Do not rely on this, but arrange a meeting with your child's new teacher at the beginning of each year. At the meeting explain your child's difficulties and give the teacher copies of any assessments done in the past.

During the year, keep in regular contact with the teacher to find out how your child is progressing. It is a good idea for the child's homework diary to be used as a 'communication book' in which you and the teacher can exchange information on a regular basis. You should not hesitate to request a special meeting with your child's teacher if there is something causing you concern. Do this as early as possible.

It is sometimes possible to apply for funding for special teaching sessions at school for a child with ADHD. These may be given in the class or in a resource room. The child may receive individual help, or be part of a small group of children with similar difficulties. If you think this may be possible, check with your child's teacher to see whether it is available. Some schools have an arrangement whereby parents come to the class and help children with their reading or other work.

Try not to become involved in discipline issues that should be the domain of the school. If a child is misbehaving at school, the teachers, possibly with the aid of the principal, should develop strategies for dealing with this. The school may need to call upon a psychologist attached to the school if such expert advice is needed.

As a parent, it is probably best if you are not put in the position of having to punish your child for misdemeanors at school. This only increases stresses at home and creates negative interactions between parent and child. While you should always be prepared to go to the school at the teacher's request to discuss behavioral problems, you should try wherever possible to encourage the school to deal with these problems, while you deal with the behavior problems you observe at home. Often the best role for a parent of a child who is behaving badly at school is to provide him with a happy home environment where he is given unconditional love. In this way behavior at school may improve as the child's self-esteem is built up.

13
School management

The average school-age child spends well over a third of her time in school. A child's experiences in the classroom, and in the playground, will affect her academic attainments, the development of her self-esteem, and her social skills. Since these are the areas where children with ADHD have difficulties, it is essential that teachers and principals understand how best to help children with this common disability.

In the past, teachers often had little understanding of the needs of a child with ADHD. Such children were labeled as 'lazy' or 'bad', and often dealt with harshly. Problems with learning and social skills were not detected early and children were not assessed adequately. Parents were often blamed for their child's difficulties. Those parents who arranged for their child's difficulty to be properly assessed and diagnosed often found that teachers and principals had never heard of ADHD. Educational programs were not implemented and the school could be uncooperative with medication regimes.

Now there is a growing awareness of ADHD within the education system. Teachers are increasingly being taught about ADHD in their university training and in-service courses. Many education departments have produced guidelines and information booklets about ADHD for teaching staff.

The interested teacher can also gain access to a number of books written about ADHD especially for teachers. These include books such as 'The ADHD Hyperactivity Handbook for Schools' by Harvey C. Parker and 'Attention Without Tension: A Teacher's Handbook on Attention Disorders' by Copeland and Love. These are books written for teachers by specialist teachers and psychologists. There are also many videos that give an insight into appropriate teaching techniques. These include 'Educating Inattentive Children', by Samuel and Michael Goldstein, and 'ADHD in the Classroom: Strategies for Teachers', by Russell Barkley.

For teachers who want to understand how best to help a child with ADHD, there are now many sources of information and special teaching materials. All these books, videos, and teaching materials may be ordered from the ADD WareHouse (see Appendix for website address).

Unfortunately, there are still teachers who are ignorant of ADHD. Many of these teachers will be eager to become informed about ADHD when they realize that they have a child in their class with the condition. Other teachers, a decreasing minority, will claim that they 'do not believe in ADHD', or that they are 'against' certain treatments such as medication. Such teachers may prefer to blame parents for the child's difficulties, claim that the child is lazy, or believe that punishing the child will remedy the problem. They may have misconceptions about the role of medication in this disorder and be ignorant of the literature on ADHD. Some have a misconception that all children with ADHD are constantly active, and do not understand the wide range of difficulties seen in children with this condition.

Which school?

Choosing a child's school usually requires some degree of compromise on the part of the parents. Whatever placement you eventually decide upon, it is unlikely to be perfect. Schools rarely are. What you need to find is the best alternative for your child at that stage of her education. Always keep in mind that no placement needs to be permanent. Regular reviews should be undertaken, and your child could move to a more appropriate class or school if her needs are found to have changed.

All things being equal, a child is usually best placed at a school that is near to her home. Besides making transportation easier, it also gives the child an opportunity to meet and mix with neighborhood children with whom she will be able to play after school.

It is essential that the principal of the school has a good understanding of ADHD. This means that he or she should know about the condition, have an enlightened attitude toward comprehensive assessment, and be prepared to implement a multi-modal treatment plan which includes behavior management, special educational help, and medication. If the principal does not understand ADHD, it is going to be extremely difficult to ensure that the child receives appropriate help.

The classes in the school should preferably not be too large. It is very difficult for one teacher to help a child with ADHD if there are more than 30 children in the class. Classrooms should be closed spaces (not open plan). Seating should be in rows with children facing the teacher, rather than with desks placed in small clusters.

The school should be structured with clear-cut rules that children can understand. School programs that allow children to come and go as they please and to choose which activities they want to take part in are often not appropriate for children with ADHD.

Children should be in classes grouped by age so that they have a feeling of belonging with their peer group. Composite classes and 'Vertical streaming' systems are usually confusing and distracting for most children with ADHD.

It is best if children are streamed according to ability for each individual subject. This allows children who are weaker in a particular subject to receive extra help and to work at an appropriate pace. It also enables a child to have the satisfaction of moving up to a higher stream as she improves.

The school should employ support teachers for children with learning difficulties so that they can receive extra help within the ordinary class.

The classroom teacher should understand ADHD and be able to implement the strategies discussed below for helping children who are experiencing difficulties.

Effective strategies for teaching children with ADHD

Diagnosis and assessment first

It is essential that a child who is experiencing difficulties in the classroom or the playground should first have an adequate assessment before any management plan is formulated. Such an assessment involves a developmental pediatrician and psychologist as discussed in Chapter 11.

No management plan should be devised until such an assessment has been carried out to establish the child's particular strengths and difficulties and to identify the cause or causes of the child's problems.

Teachers' attitudes

To properly manage a child with ADHD, a teacher must have an understanding of what it is like to be a child with ADHD. The teacher should also have some insight into his or her own make-up and response to the child. Some teachers have a natural ability to empathise with children who have ADHD, and find it easy to get the best out of such children. Other teachers may find that they become very angry and frustrated with children with ADHD and that their natural teaching style, which may be successful with children who do not have this condition, is not suitable for children with ADHD.

A teacher who feels frustrated by the difficulties presented by a child with ADHD, who finds it difficult to carry out a behavior management program or make classroom adjustments for the child with ADHD, should turn to the school psychologist. With regular consultation with the psychologist, the teacher should be able to gain insight into his or her difficulties and develop better strategies for overcoming these.

Classroom accommodation

It is important that the teacher should create a proper learning environment for the child with ADHD. The child with ADHD should be seated in the front of the class near to the teacher's desk. The teacher should ensure that the child's seat is part of the regular class seating and not separate from the other children. By placing her at the front, the teacher can ensure that he or she has the child's attention. This position also has the advantage that the child with ADHD will have her back to the rest of the class so that other students are less likely to distract her. The old idea of putting the 'naughty' child at the back of the class, or letting such a child seat herself at the back of the class, is totally inappropriate if the child has ADHD.

It is a good idea to place children who will serve as good role models on either side of the child with ADHD. Example is the greatest teacher and the child with ADHD will benefit from copying the behavior of the children around her, and will also be less distracted by them if they are well-behaved and have good work habits. The teacher can make the most of the proximity of these good role models by encouraging peer teaching and cooperative learning.

Wherever possible, the teacher should keep the child with ADHD away from distracting stimuli. The child should be seated well away from distractions such as an air-conditioner or window.

Children with ADHD do need to be in an interesting environment, but the teacher should avoid creating a learning environment that is too 'busy'. Rather than filling the classroom with posters covered with information, and objects such as mobiles, the teacher should aim to make the classroom interesting but muted in tone. School bags should be placed at the back of the class out of the way, and the desks and boards should be kept uncluttered.

The playground

In the same way that it is important to provide an appropriate learning environment for the child in the classroom, it is important that the child with ADHD be adequately catered for in the playground.

Children with ADHD often need supervision in the playground so that they do not cause problems to themselves or others. This supervision should be carried out in such a way that the child with ADHD does not feel she is being singled out.

If the child with ADHD wishes to play with younger children in the playground, this should be allowed. Often children with ADHD have more in common with younger children and feel happiest in that social setting. Provided that they are not causing any disruption or harm, they should be allowed to play with any child.

If a child with ADHD is having difficulties getting on with other children, it is useful to arrange for the school psychologist to talk to her about effective strategies for getting on with other children. It may be very difficult for the child with ADHD to apply these strategies, but such intervention may pay great dividends.

Children with ADHD usually benefit from individualized activities that are non-competitive. Many do not do well in team sports. The child may be encouraged to take part in games such as t-ball and trampoline if these suit her abilities.

Working with parents as a team

The teacher of a child with ADHD should keep in regular contact with the child's parents. Sometimes this is best done through a communication book or the child's school diary. For confidential matters, a special meeting should be arranged.

The aim of the parent–teacher communication is to ensure that everyone is aware of how the child is progressing and what steps are being taken to help the child in the school and home environments. It also gives teachers an opportunity to speak to parents about ways of helping the child with her work at home. Teachers can encourage parents to help the child with her study and to review completed homework.

It also allows the teacher to suggest whether remedial help is needed after school.

Parents can play a role in ensuring that their child's books and bag are organized and that particular difficulties with homework are conveyed to the teacher.

Parents should not have to punish children for misdemeanors at school. Parents should also not have to punish children for homework that is not done. Although many educators favor what is known as 'a home and school-based contingency program' (where the parents administer rewards and consequences at home, based upon a teacher's assessment), such programs are inappropriate for most, if not all, children with ADHD.

There are a number of drawbacks to home and school-based contingency programs. First, children with ADHD have a lot of difficulty delaying gratification long enough to receive rewards at home for behavior at school. Second, it seems inappropriate that a child who has been well-behaved at home, but had a bad day at school, should be punished by his parents. By rights, parents should, in this situation, be rewarding the child for his good home behavior. Third, children with ADHD are unreliable about bringing teacher's report cards home. A further problem with such programs is that, because parents are not present at school, they are at a great disadvantage if the child wants to defend her actions at school. Parents cannot be sure whether the behavior was misinterpreted, misunderstood, or was a reasonable response to provocation. It is, therefore, the teacher's role to monitor behavior at school and to deal with this appropriately.

Giving instructions

Children with ADHD have poor listening skills and it is important that teachers understand how to give instructions to their students with ADHD.

First it is important to gain the child's attention. It is usually necessary to stand in front of the child, and even to touch the child, in order to ensure that she is able to listen to you. Do not insist that the child looks at you, however, as children with ADHD often have low self-esteem and find it difficult to maintain eye contact. To force the child to look at you may only make her feel extremely uncomfortable so that she is unable to concentrate on what you are saying. Unfortunately, some teachers regard a child's failure to look at them as rudeness and punish such children. Teachers should not say things such as, 'Look at me when I am talking to you!' to a child with ADHD. Children who avert their gaze, or look downward, may not be rude at all: simply embarrassed and uncomfortable.

The instructions should be as brief and clear as possible. Avoid giving instructions that contain a number of different parts, such as 'Go to the back of the class, open your bag, and take out your maths book!'. It would be more appropriate to simply say 'Go to your bag', and then, only when the child is at her bag, to say 'Take out your maths book'. Children with ADHD have problems with short-term memory and find it very difficult to retain a two- or three-part instruction.

It is always important to ensure that the child understands an instruction before beginning the task. It may be necessary to repeat the instruction. This should be done in a friendly, calm manner.

Unfortunately, many children with ADHD do not ask for help and a teacher should always try to create an environment where the child with ADHD will feel comfortable seeking assistance.

Children with ADHD often have difficulty carrying out instructions because of their poor organization skills. It may be necessary for children to have all books for a particular subject color coded. They may need a list of the steps required to carry out instructions.

It is essential that teachers ensure that the child is supervised when writing down her homework and that parents know how to check this work. A child with ADHD who is asked to do a task should have regular monitoring to ensure that she knows what is expected and whether she is succeeding.

With all instructions, the teacher should ensure that the child is actually capable of carrying out the task and that it is not beyond her abilities.

Modifying work and examinations for the child with ADHD

Teachers should ensure that children with ADHD are tested on their knowledge and not unfairly penalised for their difficulties with concentration.

It is important not to overload the child with tasks that need a great deal of persistence. For example, it may be necessary to shorten the work so that the child only does every second mathematics problem.

When setting out questions for the child, these should be given in 'bite size' sections, rather than giving the child a page filled with questions.

The tasks should be broken up into smaller stages, each one on a separate piece of paper; each sheet is then given to the child separately.

It may be important for the teacher to consult with the school counsellor, or special education teacher, to modify assignments and homework according to the child's particular areas of strength and weakness. The development of an individualized education program for the child may be necessary.

It may be best to give the child extra time to finish examinations. Children with ADHD are easily frustrated and do poorly under the stress of an examination. They also find it very difficult to write down their thoughts on paper and usually do better in a multiple-choice examination than in the essay type.

In any examination, it is important that the teacher be available to answer queries. Children with ADHD are less likely to seek assistance and it may be important for the teacher to keep an eye on what the child is doing in a discreet way, so as to be able to guide the child if she has misunderstood the question.

Behavior management

In the next chapter behavior modification for parents is described. Teachers can implement the same sort of programs with children who have specific behaviors that are causing difficulties.

It is essential that a teacher be able to talk to a child with ADHD in private, in order to discuss ways in which the child may be helped. The teacher should be able to take the child aside in a way that is not obvious to the other children in the class and be able to discuss areas of behavior that are a problem. This should be done calmly so that child and teacher can develop some strategies together. Clear consequences for misbehavior should be established from the outset. The methods of monitoring the behavior should be discussed. Discipline should always be appropriate to the misdemeanor and not unnecessarily harsh. Reasonable allowance should also be made for periods of difficulty.

It should always be remembered that children with ADHD manage transitions very poorly and some allowance should be made for this. Such transitions include periods when they come into the classroom after breaks, when they move from one classroom to another, or when they have a new teacher. They are liable to become over-excited when they are due to have some activity that they enjoy, such as an outing or a sports event, and this should also be taken into consideration.

In all situations, the teacher should aim to help the child's self-esteem. Ridicule and criticism should always be avoided. Rewards should be used liberally in order to help build up the child's self-esteem. Rewards should be given as soon as possible after wanted behavior has been demonstrated. Teach the child to reward herself by encouraging positive self-talk ('You finished the job very well. How do you feel about that?'). This sort of cognitive re-structuring encourages the child to be more positive about herself.

Wherever possible try to encourage the child to monitor herself. This teaches her self-control. Self-monitoring requires that the student observes her own behavior and records the observations. For example, a child can be given a checklist in which she is asked to mark whether she was paying attention whenever she hears a beep on a tape. A commercially available program, 'The Listen, Look and Think Program' (Impact Publications Inc.), is available. It is helpful for the student to compare her ratings with those of the teacher.

Extra help for children with ADHD

Children with ADHD are often behind in one or more areas of academic attainment. They may therefore need some individualized help. Children with ADHD usually learn very well in a one-to-one situation and may make rapid strides if given some individualized attention.

Teachers may be able to find time during the school day when they can sit down with the child and provide help on a one-to-one basis. If this is not available, or if the teacher cannot provide sufficient help in this way, it is important to look for other ways of giving the child such assistance.

Schools may be able to fund a special needs teacher who provides help on a one-to-one basis to children with learning difficulties. If this is not available, the teacher should consider whether a volunteer can provide this kind of help. Such volunteers may be parents or senior citizens. A good teacher will know how to utilize a volunteer in the classroom. This may be through training the volunteer to give one-to-one help, or by letting the volunteer take over some other chore so that the teacher can spend more individual time with the child who has ADHD. Volunteers do need to be trained and supervised and should be treated in a professional manner. They need to be made aware that all information pertaining to a student must be treated in a confidential manner.

When children are clearly unable to receive sufficient help for their difficulties in the classroom, teachers should advise parents to arrange for extra help outside of school hours. With so many children in most classes, it is often necessary for children with learning difficulties to receive help from a tutor on a regular basis after school. It is best if the classroom teacher ensures that such help is appropriate.

The teacher may be able to recommend an appropriate tutor. He or she should be prepared to meet with the tutor to ensure that work in the classroom can be reinforced by the tutor. It is essential that the tutor should make the child's schoolwork easier for him, and not add extra or different work for the child to do.

The teacher and the child's medication

Teachers have an important role in supervising the administration of medication for children with ADHD and in monitoring the positive, as well as the negative, effects of such medication. In order to do this effectively, the teacher should understand the important role that medication plays in helping children with ADHD. The teacher who is ignorant about the potential advantages of medication in such children will not be able to take on this role.

The teacher should understand that medication is one of the components of helping the child. It is to be used together with other strategies in order to get the best results.

It is important that children who take medication for ADHD should not feel self-conscious about this. Teachers should never remind students publicly to take their medicine. In some cases children are able to supervise the administration of their medication on their own, and teachers need play no part in the actual administration. For younger and less capable children, the teacher may need to ensure, in a discreet way, that the child takes his tablet. In all schools children take medication regularly for conditions such as asthma, and it should be quite usual for children to take medicine in the classroom, or to go up to one of the staff rooms to take medication. Teachers should ensure that this can happen without any fuss.

The taking of medication should never be alluded to at other times. Certainly, a teacher should not comment on the child's performance in relation to whether medication has been taken or not.

Teachers and principals are often concerned about a child having medicine in his possession. They are concerned that some other child may get hold of the medicine and take it. First, it is not necessary for a child to have in her possession at school more than a single dose of the medicine. This is usually the tablet taken at recess or lunch. It is extremely unlikely that another child would take this tablet, but if one did, no harm would come to the other child. A single dose of any of the medicines taken for ADHD would be safer than taking a single dose of almost any other medicine used in pediatrics (including penicillin). Children should be taught from an early age not to take other people's tablets.

Teachers also have the important role of monitoring the effects of medication. There are now a number of checklists that teachers can use to tick off the effects of medication that they observe. Teachers are well placed to notice effects, both good and bad, that result from medication.

Table 7 shows a rating scale which teachers can use for this purpose. If untoward reactions are noted by the teacher, he or she should convey

Table 7 Medication effects rating scale

Behavior	Never	Occasionally	Appropriate for age
Attentive to teacher			
Persistent with work			
Inconsistent work			
Neat work			
Disruptive in class			
Accepted by peers			
Carries out instructions			
Follows routines			
Tantrums			
Stays in seat			
Rude to teacher			
Remembers work			
Tries hard			
Negative comments about self			
Obeys rules			

Side effects	Never	Mild	Severe
Staring into space			
Abnormally subdued			
Sad			
Anxious			
Headaches			
Abdominal pain			
Rebound			
Tics			

this to the parents. With the parents' permission it may be necessary for the pediatrician and teacher to discuss the effects of the medication so that the dose can be adjusted.

Sometimes, children with ADHD show an improvement in their concentration at the expense of becoming slightly subdued by the medication. In consultation with the teacher, the pediatrician can lower the dosage so that the positive effect on concentration remains, while the subduing effect of the medication disappears.

It is unfortunate that there are still many teachers and principals who are negative about medicine for ADHD. Because of this attitude, pediatricians and parents may decide not to involve the teacher in monitoring the child's medication. They may even decide not to tell the teacher that the child is taking medication for fear that he or she will react in a negative way and make the child feel uncomfortable about his treatment. In such a situation, the teacher is doing the child a great disservice. Such teachers, are, by their attitudes, disqualifying themselves from playing an important role in a vital aspect of their pupil's education.

14

Behavior modification

Behavior modification is a form of teaching that is employed in situations where explanation alone does not succeed. Most parents practise behavior modification without realizing it. They do this by rewarding their child for good behavior and punishing him for bad. Some parents need help in order to do this in the most effective way. Children benefit from knowing where they stand, and being able to direct their energies into more constructive and rewarding activities.

Step 1—identify the behavior

The first step in a behavior modification program is to observe your child's behavior and identify the behavior you want to change. You need to avoid general statements about your child such as 'he is impossible', and instead focus on specific things he does that worry or annoy you, for instance not getting dressed in the morning, or fighting with a sibling.

Step 2—what kind of behavior is it?

There are two kinds of behavior: good behavior, which you want to encourage, and undesirable behavior, which you want to get rid of. In the above examples, the good behavior you want to encourage is getting dressed in the morning and the undesirable behavior you want to get rid of is fighting with the sibling. Ideally, it is always best to teach a child a useful skill to replace an unwanted behavior. For example, if a child is fighting with siblings, try to think of an alternative behavior that the child can become involved in to replace this.

Step 3—examine antecedents and consequences

This way of looking at behavior is sometimes known as the 'ABC' method. 'A' is for antecedents, which are those triggers that encourage unwanted behavior. 'B' stands for the behavior, which needs to be carefully defined. 'C' stands for the consequences, i.e. those things that happen because of the behavior. It is important to work out which particular consequences maintain a behavior, i.e. what keeps the child behaving in this particular way.

In the above example, if every time the child with ADHD hits his sibling he receives attention from the parent, even if this attention is not good quality attention (such as shouting), this may reward and reinforce the behavior. Children enjoy attention, and if the only sort of attention they can get is negative attention, they will still continue behaving in such a way as to receive it.

Encouraging good behavior so that it can be rewarded

It is important to encourage desirable behavior, which can then be rewarded. Often children with ADHD demonstrate so little desirable behavior that parents have difficulty finding something that they can reward. Medication may play an important role in this regard in that children with ADHD may only start behaving in a desirable way once they are on medication.

One way of encouraging good behavior is to demonstrate the behavior to the child in the hope he will imitate it. Some children are more inclined to imitate behavior than others. Your child may copy the parent he identifies with more strongly, and you should take advantage of this. For example, if you want your child to sit down and do homework it may be best if the father sits down to do his work and invites the child to sit at the same table and join him. Children also tend to copy other children. It is useful to encourage your child to come into contact with good role models whom he may imitate.

Another way of encouraging good behavior is by modifying the child's environment. If a child takes a long time to dress, ensure his clothes are set out so that they are easy to put on, that the room is warm, and that there are minimal distractions.

If, as sometimes happens, the correct behavior suddenly occurs, you should take advantage of this and reward the child immediately. Be alert to 'catch' your child demonstrating a good behavior so that this can be rewarded.

How to reward good behavior

How should you reward your child? The simplest sort of reward would be to praise what the child has done by making a fuss, smiling, and saying 'well done', or 'quick dressing', or 'good reading' etc.

Note that 'good' is used to describe the behavior, not the child. This emphasizes what you are praising, and does not in any way reflect on the child's worth. These simple verbal rewards should always be given and are often more powerful than parents realize. In some cases, however, they are not enough on their own. The older the child, the less likely that this simple kind of reward will suffice. In this case, you need to provide some tangible reward. This may take the form of a star on a chart, a 'smiley' stamp on the hand, a sweet, a raisin, a special toy, or an outing. With more sophisticated children, it may be necessary to have a system where a specific number of small tokens earns something a little larger.

Beware of the trap of making the reward too big or too expensive. You should not make it too easy to get big rewards, although you should make it reasonably easy to earn lesser rewards to encourage the child.

Sometimes a reward system is best run along the lines of a 'response-cost' system where the child forfeits some tokens when unwanted behavior occurs.

Children with ADHD often benefit from a system where they initially receive all the tokens for the week, or day, so that they can see the reward from the outset. They then have to give up a certain number of tokens that they have in their possession whenever they display unwanted behavior. This works well because children with ADHD experience difficulty working toward a reward that will only become available to them at some future time.

In all cases, stamps, tokens, or charts should be available at the outset. Once the behavior modification program is in operation, you will need to revise the reward system if it is clear that the child is waiting too long for a reward, or is getting too many rewards.

Keep up this tangible reward system until the child loses interest, which he will invariably do once the desired behavior has been established for a period of time. Do keep up the praise, however, even when tangible rewards are no longer given.

How to discourage undesirable behavior

Discouraging undesirable behavior causes parents much difficulty and confusion. Without realizing it, they often reward the bad behavior, or use ineffective ways of eradicating unwanted behavior.

The most common *ineffective* method is to scold the child or to argue with him. Most parents would agree that this is not usually successful. The reason is that, for many children, any attention from their parent acts as a reward. Children thrive on attention, and always seem to want more. They prefer praise, but any attention, even scolding, can be rewarding for a child. (An analogy for this is that children usually like crisp potato chips; however, if only soggy potato chips are available, they will usually eat them.)

Some parents resort to smacking their child, but usually find that this does not help for long. This may make parents very distressed, as they regard smacking as the most extreme action they can take. The reason why smacking does not seem to work is probably because it *is* such an extreme thing to do. Although it is unpleasant for the child, it is also unpleasant for the parent and most children realize this. After the smack, parents invariably feel guilty; when the pain caused by the smack has subsided, the child may enjoy the sympathy he senses from the remorseful parent. Smacking may therefore work for the moment, but usually does not eradicate a recurrent behavior.

Pretending to ignore

What can parents do when these traditional methods do not work? Parents may need to learn that often the best thing to do is *to do nothing*. Children thrive on attention, even in the form of shouting and smacking. By withholding attention, many behaviors will diminish or disappear. Ignoring behavior is a difficult thing to do; in fact it is questionable whether parents can ever completely ignore their child's behavior. You can, however, *pretend* to ignore the behavior if it is not too dangerous or disruptive. To do this you have to stifle your natural responses, avoid making eye contact with the child, and look calm. Busy yourself with some activity unrelated to the child and refuse to become involved in any discussion or argument about the behavior that you are trying to eradicate. When the child has stopped demonstrating the particular behavior, invite him to take part in what you are doing and resume normal conversation with him. Do not show annoyance once you start interacting with him again.

Time-out

In the case of behaviors that are too destructive, or possibly dangerous, you cannot pretend to ignore your child because of the concern that he may injure himself, or damage something or someone. You may be so angry with him that you may be afraid of losing control and harming him. In such situations, you have to remove the child to a place where he can no longer receive the reward of your attention.

This technique is known as 'time-out', and consists of insisting that the child stay on his own for a while. The aim of using 'time-out' is not to create discomfort or fear in the child but simply to remove him from the place where he is receiving reinforcement for what he is doing. Usually the most convenient place for 'time-out' is the child's bedroom. Leave him there until you have both calmed down. While the child is there, any shouting or screaming should be ignored.

It is important not to allow the child out until he has quietened down, otherwise he may get the idea that he has been allowed out because of his screaming and shouting. You can either tell the child in a calm voice that you will not allow him out until he is quiet, or if he does not understand this and will not cooperate, you can wait until there is a pause in his crying and then allow him out.

Some children are so destructive in their own room that it may be necessary to pick another room in the house. Concern is sometimes expressed that, if a child spends 'time-out' in his bedroom, he will develop a bad association with it. In practice this does not seem to occur.

At the end of a period of 'time-out', do not demand an apology or engage in recriminations. Be friendly and matter-of-fact.

One should never use 'time-out' without giving some thought to the quality of interaction that you have with the child when you are together. In other words, one should not only be thinking of 'time-out', but also of 'time-in'. Wherever possible you should try to ensure that the time your child spends with you promotes positive interactions and encourages wanted behavior. You do not need to continually entertain your child or spoil him during the time he is with you. However, you need to ensure that he is getting sufficient quality time with you so that he is not forced to get your attention through undesirable behavior.

It is very easy for an exhausted and stressed parent to find that they are not giving their child good quality 'time-in'. Quality time simply implies that you are giving your child your undivided attention and that both of you are enjoying yourselves.

Brief restraint

In situations where 'time-out' cannot be used, another way of managing aggressive behavior is to firmly hold the child's arm at his sides for a count of fifteen. He is then released. If the behavior recurs, this should be repeated. This method is known as 'brief restraint'. It is not suitable for a child who is physically stronger than the parent.

When holding a child in brief restraint, you should not interact with him. The idea is to stop the pleasure of walking and running about for a few minutes, not make the restraint itself a form of positive interaction.

Extinction

There are some situations where a child becomes used to being rewarded for an unwanted behavior. An example is prolonged calling out at night that eventually results in the desired parent's appearance in the room. The withdrawal of such a reward is called 'extinction'.

There are two ways of doing this: abrupt withdrawal or gradual withdrawal. The latter is sometimes referred to as 'controlled crying' and is usually favored. In this method, you need to wait for longer and longer periods before returning to your child. The attention given to the child on your return should be minimal.

With extinction, you should be prepared for the behavior to worsen initially. This usually lasts a few days, and if you hold firm, the behavior will rapidly diminish and disappear. After a variable period, there is often a reappearance of the behavior, as if your child is testing whether the new rules still apply. If you continue to be consistent, the behavior will cease.

Before embarking on an extinction program, both the parents should prepare themselves for a trying time. During the period when the behavior worsens, it is important to support one another.

Important considerations in a behavior modification plan

Behavior modification is straightforward in theory—encourage and reward good behavior, discourage bad. In practice it can be very difficult, particularly as children reach adolescence.

First you should always take into account the fact that a child with ADHD has an inefficiency of the brain that means that he has less control over his behavior. Always assess your child's behavior and decide whether the child is *able* to change or not, given his difficulties. Your pediatrician or psychologist who carried out the diagnostic assessment will be able to guide you.

One of the great advantages of medication is that it allows children to be more successful in a behavior modification program because desirable behaviors increase and unwanted behaviors decrease.

You should be as consistent as possible. Decide on the limits of what your child may and may not do, and then try to stick to them. Complete consistency is, of course, impossible, but aim for as much consistency as possible. You should not be discouraged if others do not set the same limits as you do. Children with ADHD can accept different limits from different people. What confuses them is when one person acts inconsistently.

Always ask yourself if some practical change would make a behavior easier to manage. This may be simpler than embarking on a behavior management program. For example, behavior management could be tried with a child who continually enters an older brother's or sister's bedroom and untidies it. However, the easiest way to resolve the problem may be to put a bolt and combination lock on the sibling's door that can be opened and locked by the sibling, but not by the child with ADHD. Sometimes parents resist such an approach because they feel they do not want their home to feel like a prison. This may be preferable to a home that feels like a battlefield!

A child with ADHD who cannot resist taking chocolate bars from the grocery cupboard because of his insatiability and poor impulse control, may be controlled by the installation of child-proof locks, or by hiding the chocolates. Sometimes parents are so close to the problem, and under so much stress, that they find it difficult to stand back and think of these practical solutions.

Many children with ADHD demonstrate a number of unwanted behaviors. You will need to decide which you want to tackle first. It is usually only possible to successfully tackle one behavior at a time. Sometimes the choice is easy; the most worrying behavior may be the most amenable to change. Sometimes behaviors are related, and eradicating one may get rid of others. If you are feeling overwhelmed by a number of behavior problems, it may be more rewarding to tackle a relatively minor problem first. Your quick success may then encourage you to tackle the bigger problems.

Do not ignore your own stress. It is very difficult to manage a child's behavior when you are at breaking point. Children with ADHD can be extremely stressful to parents because they do not obey reasonable rules, and the behavior of a difficult child can create tremendous stress in a family and drive parents apart. Both parents need a chance to express their feelings about the child. There are times when you need to get away and have a break. It may be a matter of having your child minded while you go for a walk, listening to some music, or soaking in a warm bath.

The basis of many of the undesirable behaviors in children with ADHD is poor self-esteem. Often children behave poorly at home because of negative experiences at school with their peers or a teacher. If these antecedents are understood, much can be done to decrease behaviors by building up the child's self-esteem, as discussed in Chapter 12.

Some children behave less well as they become tired at the end of the day, and this may also need to be taken into consideration.

Some children may have behavior difficulties because their medicine is not covering the entire waking period. Sometimes children's behavior may become worse as the medicine wears off, an effect known as 'rebound'. For this reason, difficulties in a child's behavior should always be discussed with your child's pediatrician.

In many children the onset of puberty is associated with worsening of behavior. Although puberty is a time when the brain may mature and the ADHD resolve, for some this does not happen and the only effect of puberty is the worsening of behavior due to the effect of the hormones on the brain. Parents often do not realize that the hormonal changes associated with puberty start some 2–3 years before the physical changes are seen in the body. Knowing that the behaviors are due to the hormonal effects of puberty may make you feel more able to bear them. In most children, this difficult phase will usually pass when the initial rapid changes of puberty are over.

Many parents find it difficult to plan and implement a behavior management program on their own. If, after trying the methods described above, you have not succeeded, do not hesitate to consult your doctor and ask for a referral to a psychologist. A psychologist will spend time finding out about the child's behavior and also about the home situation. He or she will then be able to plan, with your help, what you need to do to modify the behavior. He or she will keep in contact with you and provide advice if further problems arise.

15
Medicines—general principles

As explained in Chapter 10, evidence from many sources points to low levels of neurotransmitters in the frontal part of the brain as the cause of ADHD.

On the basis of this evidence, the ideal treatment for ADHD would be a medicine that increased the amount of these neurotransmitters to levels appropriate for the child's age. Fortunately, several such medicines exist.

In every child with ADHD, consideration should be given to the use of one of these medicines as part of the treatment. Ideally, such a medicine would be administered to the child from an early age, before problems with poor self-esteem, social difficulties, academic failure, and family stress have caused irreversible harm. In a child who is receiving an appropriate medicine, all other forms of treatment, such as educational and psychological intervention, will be more effective.

These medicines help the child's brain to function like the brains of other, normal children; they do not sedate the child. Most, but not all, children will be helped by medication.

While the effects of these medicines last only as long as the medicine remains in the child's body, any skills the child has learned will persist. This means that children who are treated with medication have better academic outcomes and fewer long-term behavioral and emotional complications from their ADHD than those who do not. In addition, as explained in Chapter 10, there is now research that suggests that individuals with ADHD who are treated with medication during childhood may be more likely to grow out of their condition during late puberty than those who are not.

How do the medicines work?

All the medicines used to treat ADHD increase the amount of one or both of the neurotransmitters dopamine and norepinephrine.

Each acts on one or more of the steps involved in the release, re-uptake, breakdown, and autoregulation of these neurotransmitters at the nerve ending (synapse).

Figure 9 is a schematic representation of these steps, which were described in Chapter 10.

Table 8 lists the medicines used in the treatment of ADHD and their site of action. Some of the medicines act at several points in the synapse, but only the most important action in ADHD is listed in the table.

Precisely where each medicine acts has been discovered by research in biochemical pharmacology, the study of how medicines change the chemistry of the body. For example, because the action of methylphenidate (Ritalin) is blocked by the drug reserpine, while that of dexamphetamine is not, differences between the action of Ritalin and dexamphetamine can be studied. Reserpine depletes dopamine and norepinephrine from storage vesicles, indicating that one of the ways that Ritalin acts is by releasing these neurotransmitters from the storage vesicles.

Some medicines used in ADHD are also used for other conditions, but treatment of ADHD requires smaller doses. These medicines have different effects on the neurotransmitter pathway in different doses.

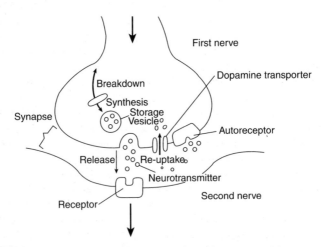

Figure 9 The pathway of neurotransmitter release, re-uptake, and breakdown at the synapse. The autoreceptor, responsible for feedback, and the dopamine transporter, responsible for re-uptake, are also shown.

Table 8 How medicines used in ADHD increase levels of dopamine and/or norepinephrine in the synapse

Medication	Major action in ADHD
Methylphenidate (Ritalin)	Blocks dopamine transporter
Dexamphetamine	Releases dopamine from storage vesicles
Imipramine (Tofranil)	Inhibits re-uptake of norepinephrine
Clonidine (Catapres)	Blocks norepinephrine autoreceptors
Atomoxetine (Strattera)	Inhibits re-uptake of norepinephrine
Moclobemide (Aurorix)	Inhibits breakdown of dopamine and norepinephrine by monoamine oxidase
Risperidone (Risperdal)	Blocks dopamine autoreceptors

For example, low doses of Tofranil (imipramine) are used to treat ADHD, and increase the amount of norepinephrine in the synapse by reducing its re-uptake by the nerve cell. The same medicine is used in larger doses to treat depression, where its action on the re-uptake of another neurotransmitter, serotonin, is responsible for its antidepressant effect.

The information in Table 8 suggests that a specific medicine that helps one child with ADHD may not help another child, depending on which particular step in the neurotransmitter pathway is defective.

This has been found to be the case. Some children with ADHD are helped by only one particular medicine. Other children are helped by a number of medicines.

These individual responses probably depend on which part of the neurotransmitter pathway is affected. For example, a child who has excessive re-uptake of dopamine by the dopamine transporter would be helped by Ritalin, which blocks this step of the neurotransmitter pathway. By contrast, a child who breaks down dopamine excessively would be helped by moclobemide, which acts by inhibiting this step.

The action of a medication used to treat a child does not have to correct the precise defect in dopamine metabolism in that child; its effect can be less specific. For example, a child who has a genetic defect that makes her dopamine receptors abnormal and less responsive to dopamine may be helped by any medicine that increases the amount of dopamine. The increased levels of dopamine would flood the receptor to such a degree that it would respond. It is for this reason that the particular medication that the child responds to cannot be used to determine her precise genetic defect.

As more research is carried out, the links between specific defects in neurotransmitter metabolism and response to particular medications will be better understood. This has already begun. For example, it has been shown that children who inherit two copies of the 10 repeat variant of the DAT1 gene (described in Chapter 10) respond poorly to the medication, Ritalin. Ritalin acts by binding on to the dopamine transporter and if this is grossly abnormal, as it is in these children, Ritalin will not be able to work.

All these medicines play their role by enabling the child to have normal (or near-normal) levels of neurotransmitter, until such time as her nerve cells are capable of producing adequate levels on their own.

How do we know which is the right medicine for a particular child?

The medicine for a particular child needs to be selected with care, based on a number of considerations.

First, there is the pattern of difficulties experienced by the child. Children with oppositional behavior, for example, usually benefit from clonidine. Children with depression usually benefit from imipramine or moclobemide.

Second, there may be reasons to avoid (contraindications to) certain medicines. For example, Tofranil should be avoided in a child with an irregularity in his or her heartbeat.

After these two considerations have been taken into account, a suitable medicine is chosen and the child's response to the medicine is tested. The most thorough way of carrying this out is by means of a two-stage trial.

The two-stage medicine trial

Stage 1

This stage involves comparing the child's performance on a standardized test of concentration and memory before and after taking the medicine. This is usually carried out in the pediatrician's rooms.

This first stage of the trial is important because some children's learning deteriorates after they take a medicine that is unsuitable for them, even though their behavior may improve. The first-stage testing also allows certain side effects to be detected early, and can be used to determine the most appropriate dosage.

Computerized testing provides a very precise measure of performance and is often used for first-stage testing. Children enjoy this kind of testing as it is similar to a computer game.

First, a standardized test is administered to the child. She then takes a dose of the medicine to be evaluated and waits for an hour until the medicine has been absorbed. A second test is then administered which is different from, but of equal difficulty to, the first.

There are many factors that can affect a child's performance over a short time period, and the results of a first-stage trial should be interpreted with care.

If the child's performance on the second test is worse than on the first, this is known as an adverse response. If an adverse response occurs, a first-stage trial with another medicine, or with a different dose of the same medicine, is usually necessary.

If there is a statistically significant improvement after the medicine, this is known as a positive response. The child should then embark on a second-stage trial with that medicine.

Stage 2

The second-stage trial of the medicine occurs in the home and/or school environment. There are many rating scales that can be used to evaluate the child's performance in these situations.

For school evaluation of medicine, it is best if the teacher monitors the child's performance without knowing when the child is on medicine.

Over a period of 4 weeks, the medicine is given according to a schedule known only to the doctor and parents. During this time the teacher keeps a daily record of the child's behavior using a rating scale such as that shown in Table 7.

At the end of the period, the parents and teacher compare the teacher's ratings with the pattern of administration of the medicine. If the medicine is helpful, the child's behavior and learning should show significant improvement on the treatment days. With adequate explanation by the doctor, the teacher should be prepared to take part in this kind of trial.

Which aspects of ADHD do the medicines help?

Few groups of medicine have been subjected to as much research as those used in ADHD. The majority of the studies have focused on methylphenidate (Ritalin), but there have been many evaluations of the other medicines in the group as well.

This research has measured a number of treatment outcomes. It has involved objective measurements of children's performance, as well as the subjective ratings by parents, teachers, and peers. The studies have shown that when children with ADHD take an appropriate medicine, the improvement is wide-ranging.

Table 9 lists a small sample of the many studies that have demonstrated improvement in children with ADHD when taking medicine.

Table 9 Some examples of the beneficial effects of medicine in ADHD

Improved classroom learning
Balthazor, Wagner, and Pelham: Journal of Abnormal Child Psychology 1991, vol. 19: pages 35–52.

Improved academic productivity and accuracy
Douglas, Barr, O'Neill, and Britton: Journal of Child Psychology and Psychiatry 1988, vol. 29: pages 453–475.

Improved perceptual efficiency
Rappaport, DuPaul, Stoner, and Jones: Journal of Clinical Child Psychology 1986, vol 54: pages 334–341.

Improved short-term memory
Swanson, Kinsbourne, Roberts, and Zucker: Pediatrics 1978, vol 61: pages 21–29.

Improved vigilance, concentration, and learning
Gadow, Children on Medication, Volume 1, Little, Brown and Co, Boston 1986.

Improved quality of interaction with parents
Barkley, Karlsson, Strzelecki, and Murphy: Journal of Consulting and Clinical Psychology 1984, vol. 52: pages 750–758.

Improved response to a behavior modification program
Gittelman, Abikoff, Pollack, Klein, Katz, and Mattes in: Hyperactive Children: The Social Ecology of Identification and Treatment Academic Press, New York 1980.

Improved quality of interaction with teachers and peers
Pelham, Bender, Caddell, Booth, and Moore: Archives of General Psychiatry 1985, vol 42: pages 948–952.

Less restless and more 'normal' in class
Barkley and Cunningham: American Journal of Orthopsychiatry 1979, vol 49: pages 491–499.

Table 9 (contd)

Less aggressive

Gadow, Nolan, Sverd, Sprafkin, and Paolicelli: Journal of the American Academy of Child and Adolescent Psychiatry 1990, vol 29: pages 710–718.

Less negative and disruptive in the classroom and playground

Pelham, Bender Caddell, Booth, and Moore: Archives of General Psychiatry 1985, vol 42: pages 948–952.

Improved standing among classmates and greater social acceptance

Whalen, Henker, and Dotemoto: Child Development 1981, vol 58: pages 816–828.

More likely to be rated as 'best friend' or 'fun' by peers

Whalen, Henker, Burhmester, Hinshaw, Huber, and Laski: Journal of Consulting and Clinical Psychology 1989, vol 57: pages 545–549.

Better sporting performance

Pelham, McBurnett, Harper, Milich, Murphy, Clinton, and Thiele: Journal of Consulting and Clinical Psychology 1990, vol 58: pages 130–133.

Improved sleep quality

Kooij, Middlekoop, van Gils, Buitelaar: Journal of Clinical Psychiatry 2001, vol 62: pages 952–956.

Improved handwriting legibility

Tucha, Lange: Journal of Abnormal Child Psychology 2001, vol 29: pages 351–356.

Less alcohol and drug abuse

Wilens, Faraone, Biederman, Gunawardene: Pediatrics 2003, vol 111: pages 179–185.

Learning

A large number of studies have found that medicine enhances performance on measures of vigilance, fine-motor coordination, impulsivity, and reaction time. Positive effects have also been obtained on measures of learning and memory, both for non-verbal and verbal material.

Studies have shown that children become better at simple and complex learning procedures. They are better able to remember words and symbols they have learned. They can recall information they have learned more rapidly and more accurately.

None of the learning that occurs in children on medicine is 'state dependent'. This means that skills and knowledge acquired while a child is on medicine do not wear off when the medicine is no longer taken.

There is also a common misconception that Ritalin saps a child's creative thinking. Funk and Chessare, in a study published in the journal 'Pediatrics', in 1993, showed that Ritalin does not adversely influence creative thinking.

Studies have also shown that medicine can improve academic productivity and accuracy in children with ADHD. Handwriting becomes neater and task persistence improves.

Behavior

Medicine also results in dramatic effects on behavior. There is improvement in concentration on assigned tasks. Children on medicine are more settled and less overactive. They become less impulsive and disruptive. They become more compliant. Aggression is markedly reduced.

A common fear is that the use of medicine will make the child overly compliant and take away her natural exuberance and sparkle. This is not the case. While children with ADHD do become better able to conform to reasonable rules when taking medicine, they nevertheless remain slightly more active and impulsive than their peers. Medicine certainly does not transform them into anergic automatons.

Social skills

Medicine also helps children with their social interactions. Negative behaviors are reduced and children become less defiant. Interactions with peers improve greatly. Children are less likely to behave in a 'silly', immature, and over-excited manner. In one study, peers consistently rated children with ADHD as being more 'fun' when they were on their medicine. This observation was made without the peers knowing when the children with ADHD were on their medicine.

Emotional state

The medicines also have an effect on children's mood. Children generally become more positive about themselves and more confident in day-to-day activities. Parents report that their children become more reasonable and that outbursts of anger decrease in frequency and intensity.

Many parents have observed that their child became more outgoing and more communicative on medication.

The place of medicine in the treatment of ADHD

Medicine has the potential to reduce many of the difficulties experienced by children with ADHD. In many children, the change is dramatic. It is not unusual for the change in the child to be described as 'miraculous'. Often the child seems to be completely transformed when on treatment. This is because the child is able to behave in a more mature, age-appropriate manner.

For some children, medicine may so improve their competence that no other form of special treatment is needed. Ordinary educational programs and average parental rearing practices are sufficient for their needs. For other children, medicine alone is not enough and must be used in conjunction with individualized educational and behavior management programs.

Not every child will respond to these medicines; some 5% of children are not helped by any of the medicines currently available.

The decision about whether a child should take medication should be made by the parents on the advice of their child's pediatrician. This should follow a comprehensive assessment, as outlined in Chapter 11. Whenever possible, the child should be involved in the decision as well.

Can children with ADHD be treated adequately without medication?

Some children with mild ADHD can manage to overcome their difficulties with non-medical intervention. However, for children with moderate or severe ADHD, behavior management and educational strategies are inadequate when used alone. Why is this the case?

Behavior modification is based on rewarding desirable behavior and ignoring undesirable behavior. This is often impractical in children with ADHD, because desirable behavior is too infrequently displayed to allow reinforcement. Undesirable behavior, on the other hand, may be so disruptive or dangerous that it cannot be ignored.

The memory and attention of many children with ADHD are so impaired that they do not benefit adequately from educational programs, without the help of medication.

Another problem with non-medical treatments for ADHD is that, in situations where parents and teachers are not able to be present, the child may fail miserably. For example, in her social interactions (when adults cannot play a role) the child with ADHD may have a great deal of trouble because of her poor social cognition. This is often compounded by peers responding in a way that is detrimental to the child.

When she needs to occupy herself, or organize her work independently, the child with ADHD often becomes dysfunctional because she lacks the necessary self-direction and self-organization skills. In these situations, the child with ADHD may enter a vicious cycle. She fails because of her difficulties and then does not want to try again because she fears further failure.

Medication offers the child with ADHD the opportunity to escape this vicious cycle and enter what might be called a 'virtuous cycle'. Because the child becomes more competent when taking the medicine, other forms of treatment, such as behavior modification and education programs, become more effective. With the medicine playing its role, there is a reduction in undesirable behavior. The child can therefore receive more appropriate praise. She also becomes more attentive during class and remedial work and her learning improves.

As the child becomes more successful, both at home and in school, she is prepared to attempt new tasks and to face new challenges. As she succeeds in these, her learning and behavior improve. It is not surprising, therefore, that children with ADHD often surge ahead once on medicine.

Studies such as the huge MTA trial (Multimodal Treatment of ADHD), carried out by the National Institute of Mental Health in the USA, have demonstrated that the best results are obtained by combining medicine with other strategies: the 'multi-modal' approach.

Explaining the role of medicine to your child

For the best results, it is essential that your child understands the role of the medicine.

First, emphasize to your child that she *is* able to concentrate, but that this requires a great deal of effort on her part. It is essential that she realizes that she does have the ability to concentrate, and that she does not feel that the medicine will be used because she is unable to do this at all. Explain that the role of the medicine is to make it easier for her to concentrate.

The analogy of wearing glasses (spectacles) is useful. Explain that in the same way some children wear glasses to make seeing easier, some children need medicine to make concentrating easier. Emphasize that in the same way that glasses do not dictate what the wearer should look at, so the medicine will not control what she concentrates on. She will still have to decide what she wants to concentrate on; the medicine will allow her to do this more effectively, with greater ease, and for longer periods of time.

Explain also that when one puts on a pair of glasses, one does not instantly acquire knowledge. Similarly, the tablets contain no knowledge, they will only help her to learn more effectively. She will still need to complete her work and to commit it to memory. The medicine is only an aid.

A child with ADHD embarking on treatment with medicine needs to know that her progress will be carefully monitored and that she will be given a guide as to how she is progressing. She also needs to know that the time will come when she will no longer require the medicine and that she can then stop taking it.

Most children are only too happy to have this kind of help. Some may, however, not want other children to know that they are taking medicine. Peers may say inappropriate things, and children with ADHD do not want to be teased about having to take tablets to help them. The dose that usually gives problems in this regard is the one that is taken during school hours.

If possible doses at school should be avoided. The new long-acting preparations discussed in the next chapter have been very helpful in this regard. If these are not suitable, and the child must take medication at school, it should be taken in private. For the older, more competent child, it is best if the tablet is packed with her lunch, so that she can take it during her break. The tablet can be hidden in a marshmallow, or chocolate, so that it can be swallowed without anyone else being aware. Some children take an extra plain marshmallow of a different color in case they are asked for one by a friend. These forms of harmless subterfuge are necessary to ensure that children take their medicine without drawing attention to themselves.

It is essential that all concerned, parents, teachers, and siblings, do not say things such as, 'You are behaving badly—go and take your medicine!' The taking of medicine should be a routine event, like brushing teeth; it should not attract comment.

With the intensive anti-drug campaigns directed towards children, it is not surprising that many are against the idea of regular medication. Explain that there is a great difference between a 'street drug' and a medicine prescribed by a doctor. It is not drug abuse to take a medicine prescribed for a condition by a specialist who has made a specific diagnosis and who will monitor the child's progress.

Do not have unrealistic expectations of medicine

Approximately 95% of children with ADHD are helped by medicine. The proportion of children who are helped is greater for those with the impulsive form of ADHD than those with the dreamy, vague form of the condition. In the latter group the success rate is approximately 70%.

In many children, the response to medicine is dramatic. Individuals who do not know the child is on medicine comment on how much better the child has become. If the child misses a tablet, teachers and relatives notice.

In other children, the effect is not so dramatic. Things do become easier for the child, but residual difficulties remain. In these children, medicine plays an important role, but is not the total answer to the child's difficulties.

Lastly, there is a group of children for whom medicine has no role, either because it does not help them at all, or because it actually has an adverse effect upon them. For these children, only non-medical methods of help are possible.

Medication does not cure ADHD. Nevertheless, if used appropriately as part of an overall management strategy, it plays a pivotal role in preventing irreversible difficulties in self-esteem and social and academic failure.

For those individuals whose difficulties persist into adulthood, medicine can continue to play a role in helping them to achieve their potential in their work, as well as in their social and family lives (see Chapter 18).

16

A guide to specific medicines

The medicines used in ADHD are a heterogeneous group. Their main common attribute is that they all increase neurotransmitter levels at the synapse.

Some of these medicines are used almost exclusively for treating ADHD. Others are also used for disorders as diverse as bedwetting, high blood pressure, migraines, and depression. They are generally prescribed in smaller doses for ADHD than for these other disorders.

The vast majority of children with ADHD are treated effectively with a single medicine. This is usually Ritalin (methylphenidate) or dexamphetamine. Other children need a combination of two or more medicines.

Ritalin and dexamphetamine are short-acting medicines that do not accumulate in the body. The other medicines used in ADHD act for longer and are administered in such a way as to produce a steady level in the blood stream.

This chapter deals with the main medicines used in ADHD. Ritalin and dexamphetamine are described in the greatest detail because they are most commonly used.

Not all medicines mentioned in this chapter are available in every English-speaking country. All are available in the USA and most are available in the UK, Canada, and Australia. New medicines are regularly registered in each country and you will need to check with your child's doctor about the availability of any medicine.

Stimulant medicines—Ritalin (methylphenidate) and dexamphetamine

Ritalin and dexamphetamine are related to one another; both belong to a group of medicines known as 'stimulants'. They have similar methods of action, and similar side effects.

In a normal child, Ritalin and dexamphetamine increase neuro-transmitter levels above normal, resulting in over-stimulation and over-activity: hence the name 'stimulant'. In a child with ADHD, however, they have the paradoxical effect of making the child less restless and more focused. This is because neurotransmitter levels are only increased to normal, or near normal, levels.

Although Ritalin and dexamphetamine are related, they have different effects on the neurotransmitter pathway. It is for this reason that some children respond better to one than to the other. This is the reason why medicine testing, described in the previous chapter, is so important.

Dexamphetamine was first used for children with ADHD in 1937, when Dr Charles Bradley serendipitously discovered that it helped children who had difficulties with sustained concentration. Ritalin has been used for the same purpose since 1957.

Duration of action

Both Ritalin and dexamphetamine are short-acting medicines. They take effect 1 hour after administration and their action lasts for approximately 4 hours.

In some children the effect lasts for only 3 hours, while in others it continues for 6 hours. This depends on the rapidity with which the child's body metabolizes (breaks down) the medicine, and also on how quickly the neurotransmitter levels, once raised by the medicine, are broken down in the brain.

Dosage and administration

It is best if the child takes the smallest dose of these medications required to achieve a satisfactory improvement. Some children are very sensitive to these medicines and require only a half or quarter tablet for each dose. Other children, of exactly the same body size, require one and a half or two tablets for each dose.

A 10 mg dose of Ritalin is equivalent in potency to 5 mg dose of dexamphetamine.

The appropriate dose does not depend on the child's weight and age alone. It is determined by the type of difficulties the child has, his temperament, his constitution, and the speed with which he breaks down the medicine. For example, a child who is dreamy and vague needs a relatively small dose to help his concentration and working memory. If such a child is given a larger dose, his performance may deteriorate. Children who are overactive or aggressive usually need larger doses.

Children who are delicate and anxious tolerate only small doses; robust children generally respond best to higher doses. The choice of the best dose to suit a child is as much an art as a science, and requires the prescribing doctor to have a great deal of experience in treating children with ADHD.

In all cases, it is best to start with a small dose and to then slowly increase the dose after 5 or 6 days; this enables the child to adjust gradually to the effects of the medicine.

These are not medicines that accumulate in the body, and every child will have periods during the day, as well as during the entire night, when the medicine is absent from the body. When the medicine needs to be stopped, there is no need to withdraw it slowly; the child can abruptly stop taking it.

The first dose of the day should be given with or after breakfast, because these medicines tend to decrease appetite when they are present in the body. By waiting until after breakfast, the child will not lose his appetite for this important meal.

Both of these medicines are well absorbed with food, and it is better for children to take them after food whenever possible. Pharmacists sometimes place a note on the pack saying that the tablets should be swallowed 20–30 minutes before meals. This instruction should be ignored, unless confirmed by your child's doctor, because both these medicines can suppress the child's appetite and it is best if he eats before this occurs. In addition, the medicine is more likely to cause abdominal discomfort if taken on an empty stomach.

It is usually necessary to give a second tablet some 3 hours after the first.

Although the medicine acts for approximately 4 hours, it should be remembered that the second tablet takes about an hour to work. This is why it is given 3 hours after the first.

For most children, the first tablet is given after breakfast, at approximately 7.30 a.m., and the second tablet is given at recess (little lunch), at approximately 11.00 a.m. This second tablet starts working at approximately 12.00 noon, which is when the first dose of the day has worn off.

Many children require a third dose to help with the afternoon period at home. This is important in helping the child with his homework, and also with his behavior at home. It is best if this dose is given at approximately 3.30 p.m. when the child arrives home. It should not be given later than 4.00 p.m. because it may interfere with the child's ability to fall asleep at night. Ritalin and dexamphetamine make children more alert, and this may cause insomnia.

It is often best to give a smaller amount of medicine for the third dose than for the earlier doses of the day. This has the advantage of making it easier for the child to fall asleep in the evening, and also prevents a phenomenon known as 'rebound', which may occur when the medicine abruptly wears off. 'Rebound' manifests itself by the child becoming restless or moody for a short time as the medicine suddenly stops working. The moodiness may take the form of angry outbursts or tearfulness. By giving a half dosage for the last part of the day, the effect of the medicine subsides more gradually, and so rebound does not occur.

Some children have trouble falling asleep if they are given more than two doses per day. Children on only two doses per day should take the first at approximately 8.00 a.m. and the second at approximately 12.00 noon. With this timing there is better coverage throughout the day.

An occasional child metabolizes the medicine extremely quickly and needs 4 or even 5 doses spread out through the day.

Long-term safety

The short-term safety of a medication is established by trials carried out prior to the granting of approval to market the medication. This is a prerequisite of all national drug-registering bodies. Long-term safety, however, is not established at this time.

Many lay-people have an erroneous concept about how the long-term safety of a medication is established once it has been marketed. They often believe that after a long period of time a large group of people who have taken a medicine is subjected to every conceivable test to establish if they have any signs of ill health attributable to the medicine. This is not the case.

To detect long-term side effects, we rely on treating doctors to notice and report any unusual health problems in their patients that may be attributable to a medicine they have taken. Only if a suspicion about a particular long-term side effect exists will testing for that side effect be undertaken as a research project. For this reason, the long-term safety of a medicine can best be established if a medicine has the following characteristics:

- It has been used for a long time;
- Many individuals have taken it for extended periods of time;
- It has a high public profile (i.e. it is not likely to be overlooked);
- Individuals who take it are regularly examined.

It is difficult to think of a medicine that fulfils these criteria more completely than do Ritalin and dexamphetamine. They have been used for 45 and 65 years respectively, millions of children have taken them, they are usually taken for several years, they have always had high media profiles, and individuals who have taken them have invariably been examined regularly by a specialist. In fact, Ritalin is arguably the single best-studied medicine used in pediatrics.

The only long-term side effect of Ritalin and dexamphetamine that has been reported was growth suppression, which was first noted in the 1970s. Later studies showed that this was a dose-related phenomenon, probably due to a decrease in appetite. It is a transient effect that occurs primarily in the first year of treatment, and seems to have no effect on eventual adult height. Nevertheless, the growth of children receiving these medicines should be monitored regularly by their pediatrician.

There have been no other long-term side effects reported when Ritalin and dexamphetamine have been used appropriately to treat ADHD.

Short-term side effects

Short-term side effects occur at the time that the medicine is present in the body or just as it wears off ('rebound'). Such side effects are always reversible and none is life threatening. Most are at their most severe when treatment is first commenced and decrease or disappear after the first couple of weeks of treatment. These side effects are often avoided by starting treatment with a small dose and gradually increasing to the desired dose after a few days. The side effects are as follows:

Decreased appetite   During the time that each tablet is present in the body, appetite may decrease. To prevent this side effect spoiling the child's appetite for breakfast, the first tablet of the day is usually taken after breakfast. Most children on either of these medicines usually eat slightly less during the day (a time when many school children do not eat much in any case). Most children compensate for this by eating more at the end of the day, when the effect of the medicine has worn off.

When treatment with these medicines is commenced there is often a slight loss of weight over the first couple of months. In the vast majority of children, weight stabilizes and then starts increasing again.

For many children with ADHD who are overweight, this slight drop in weight is beneficial for their self-image. It is extremely rare for loss of weight to necessitate the withdrawal of medicine. Occasionally a reduction in dose may be necessary because of weight loss.

Insomnia   The second common side effect is difficulty is falling asleep at night. This is most prominent when treatment is first started; it usually resolves after 1 or 2 weeks. If insomnia persists, the last dose of the day may be reduced or omitted. Some children are very sensitive to this effect and can only tolerate a morning dose.

Headaches and abdominal pain   An occasional child suffers from headaches or abdominal discomfort when treatment is commenced. These side effects usually disappear after a few days.

Mood changes   If a child is given an excessive dose of a stimulant medicine, he may become too focused. He may become too quiet and subdued and will lose his natural sparkle while the medicine is working. Such a child may become tearful and seem depressed when the medicine is in his body.

These responses suggest that the dose of medicine is too high for the child and should be reduced. In this situation the dose should be lowered; a child's natural exuberance should always be maintained while he is on treatment. Some children will need to have the dosage reduced by only half a tablet or less for these side effects to resolve. The tablets are scored down the middle, but can be broken into quarters, or even eighths, with a pill cutter or sharp knife. Parents should experiment with slight modifications to the dose in order to achieve the best result. They should not hesitate to contact their child's doctor if the dose does not seem to be appropriate.

Rebound   Some children might become overactive, irritable, or tearful at the time that the effects of a tablet wear off. This short-lasting phenomenon is known as 'rebound'. Some children will cope with this by becoming involved in a physical activity. Parents who realize that their child is having this reaction for a short period of time may encourage him to go outside and play, or to sit quietly and watch television. During such periods, it is important not to make excessive demands on the child. Often a half dosage of the medicine given on return from school abolishes afternoon rebound.

Special situations

Children with tics

Children who have a tendency to motor tics (see Chapter 4) may have their tics worsened by these medicines. This is not always the case, and many children's tics are unaffected, or may even improve. Nevertheless, a child with tics should be carefully monitored when taking Ritalin or dexamphetamine, and these medicines should be stopped if tics worsen. Other medicines for ADHD can then be used such as clonidine, which has the advantage of reducing tics.

Children with epilepsy

At one stage it was thought that children with epilepsy should not be given stimulant medicines. It is now realized that seizures are only in rare cases aggravated by Ritalin or dexamphetamine and these medicines can be given to most children with epilepsy.

Do Ritalin and dexamphetamine cause drug addiction?

The answer to this question is a definite 'No'. In fact, these medicines have an important advantage of protecting children with ADHD from addiction to a wide range of dependence-producing substances. Unfortunately, children with ADHD are at higher risk for substance abuse than other children because of their condition. Taking Ritalin or dexamphetamine reduces this risk to that of the normal population.

In 1999, researchers from Boston demonstrated that when children with ADHD had taken Ritalin regularly during childhood, their risk of substance abuse (to any substance) was 85% less than for children with ADHD who had not taken Ritalin (Figure 10). The same researchers have recently reported the results of their analysis of six large studies

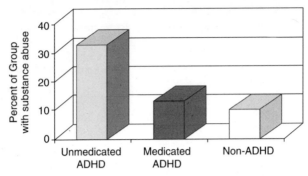

Figure 10 Treatment with Ritalin reduces substance abuse in ADHD. (Based on data from Biederman, Wilens, et al., *Pediatrics*, 1999.)

involving 1034 individuals with ADHD. This also demonstrated the protective value of stimulant medicines against later substance abuse.

Provisional data suggest that the earlier Ritalin is started in these children, the lower the risk of substance abuse.

The idea that we can 'fight drugs with drugs' is still too challenging to be promoted by the media. This important message is, therefore, not being disseminated. If it were widely known, substance abuse in the adult population may be considerably reduced.

The concern about addiction was initially raised because both methylphenidate and dexamphetamine are members of the amphetamine family. It must be emphasized that there is no risk of a child with ADHD becoming addicted to either of these medicines when they are used properly.

When amphetamines cause addiction they do so by giving the person a 'hit' or 'high' when sniffed or injected. This is due to the almost instantaneous burst of amphetamine delivered to the brain when absorbed in concentrated amounts through these routes. No such burst occurs when Ritalin or dexamphetamine are taken orally in therapeutic doses. These children do not experience a 'hit' or a 'high'. The rate of increase of dopamine generated when these medicines are taken orally is too slow to do this.

Most parents of teenagers with ADHD on Ritalin or dexamphetamine find that it is difficult to get their child to remember to take their tablets—they certainly do not ask for them or derive any pleasure from taking them.

Should Ritalin and dexamphetamine be taken on weekends?

Children whose only difficulty relates to schoolwork, need take their medicine on school days only.

An occasional child with school-based difficulties may find that he has problems falling asleep on Monday nights, because his body has to adjust to the re-introduction of the medicine after each weekend break. In such a case, it may be better for the child to take the medicine 7 days a week.

Children who have difficulties at home and at school should be given the benefit of medicine 7 days a week. For such children, their condition, and the difficulties they face, are present 7 days a week and there is no reason to withhold treatment on weekends. Taking the medicine 7 days a week allows such children's behavior to be far more consistent, and consequently they have greater opportunities to learn and succeed throughout the week.

For most children who take medicine on weekends, the dosage regime can be more flexible on Saturdays and Sundays than on other days of the week. For example, a child who takes medicine at 7.30 a.m., 11.00 a.m., and 3.30 p.m. on weekdays may find it easier to take the medicine after a late breakfast and after lunch (2 doses only) on Saturdays and Sundays.

If a child plays sport on weekends, the medicine might be given 1 hour before a game. This allows the child to be more focused during the game, and therefore more successful. (For more on stimulant medication and sport, see the next section.)

A child who has remedial lessons on weekends can also time his dose so that he takes a tablet 1 hour before the lesson. This will enable him to concentrate and persist with tasks more effectively during the lessons.

During school holidays, a child who has difficulties with behavior should be kept on his medicine unless there is a special reason to stop it, such as the need to gain weight.

Stimulant medication and sport

The effect of stimulant medication on the sporting performance of children with ADHD depends on the type of sport the child plays.

These medicines improve concentration and so improve performance in sports that require intense concentration such as baseball, cricket, and tennis. Medication may make a child with ADHD who is dreamy and uninvolved in team sports much more 'with it' and part of the game.

The medication may also be very helpful for children who cannot cooperate in coaching sessions because of their poor concentration, restlessness, and impulsive behavior.

In some contact sports, however, where aggression and impulsivity are valued (such as some football codes) these medicines may make a child too thoughtful and cautious, thereby impairing performance.

A child with ADHD whose condition undermines his ability to play sport may be tried on medication prior to an event to see if it improves or impairs his sporting performance. Children with ADHD who do not experience difficulties in sport should not take medication for sport.

Parents of children with ADHD who play sport at a high level should be aware that stimulant medicines are detected on random drug screening and are regarded as performance-enhancing drugs. It is usually permissible for these medicines to be present in the body prior to a sporting event but not during an event. They differ in this way from some other performance-enhancing drugs, such as steroids, because the effect is not to build up muscles or stamina over time, but only to improve concentration at the time that they are present in the body.

If it is necessary for the child with ADHD to take the medication during an event, it is advisable to seek written permission from the sport's governing body prior to participation. The child's doctor will need to provide a letter outlining the rationale for administering the medication and emphasizing that it is being used to correct a disability, rather than to enhance the performance of a normal child.

Traveling overseas with stimulant medication

Importation of stimulant medicines, which belong to the amphetamine family, is strictly controlled in most countries. If you intend traveling overseas and need to take your child's medication with you, seek prior information about the customs regulations in each country through which you will travel.

In most cases a letter from your child's doctor will suffice. More information may be required, particularly in those countries with significant drug trafficking problems.

Always keep a separate second copy of any documentation you receive from your doctor. A copy of the original prescription may also be helpful.

Take only the amount of medication required for the trip. Keep the tablets in their original package with the pharmacist's label stating the name of the child and the daily dosage. Keep the package insert and also take along some information about the condition, such as a book explaining it.

When to stop treatment

The decision about whether to cease the medicine should be reviewed every 6 months. Many children will continue to need their treatment until they reach the age of 16–18 years. This means that many children will need to take the medicine for several years.

Long-acting stimulant preparations

Both methylphenidate and dexamphetamine tablets act for approximately 4–6 hours. Dexamphetamine has a slightly longer duration of action than Ritalin but this is not noticeable in most children.

The standard methylphenidate and dexamphetamine tablets are 'immediate-release' or 'short-acting' forms of the medicine.

A longer lasting duration of action is often desirable and for this reason long-acting forms of these medicines have been developed.

The advantages of long-acting preparations

The child who takes a long-acting capsule in the morning does not have to take another dose at school. This is very convenient for the child and for the school staff. It is useful for children who are forgetful and for those who are embarrassed about other children knowing that they have ADHD. If other children are unaware that the child has ADHD, this prevents teasing. Concern about the adverse comments of other children is the main reason that children with ADHD do not comply with taking their medication.

Long-acting medication avoids the need for the child to miss play or lesson time in order to go to the school office or nurse's station to take the medication.

Another advantage is that a child who takes long-acting medication is not frequently reminded of his condition by the need to take tablets during the day. He is therefore less likely to feel that he is different to other children. This has a positive effect on the child's self-esteem.

When long-acting medication is taken, tablets do not have to be kept on the school premises, reducing the chance of the medication getting into the wrong hands. This reduces the chance of children without ADHD taking them accidentally or abusing them. It also puts an end to the trade in tablets that occurs in some schools. A number of long-acting forms are made in such a way that the medication cannot be extracted from the capsule and injected (mainlined) or sniffed (snorted) and so abuse is further prevented.

Long-acting forms of the medication also enable the child's teacher to monitor the effects of the medication without knowing on which days the medication has been administered (blind trial). This is the most objective way to evaluate the usefulness of the medicine in a child. As the medicine is not taken at school, it is easier for the teacher not to be involved with, or aware of, which days it has been taken.

Long-acting preparations can be very helpful for children who are rapid metabolizers of methyl-phenidate or dexamphetamine. In some children the effect of an immediate-release tablet wears off earlier than the usual lower limit of 4 hours—often after only 2 to 2.5 hours. The body of such a child is very efficient at breaking down (metabolizing) the medicine into inactive end-products.

When not to use long-acting preparations

In young children who are taking the medication to reduce poor concentration in the classroom, a long duration of action is often unnecessary because at this level of schooling most of the academic work is confined to the morning. Teachers usually do not expect young children to be able to concentrate on academic work after midday. The use of a long-acting preparation in such a child may decrease their appetite for longer than is necessary and a single immediate-release tablet before school may be preferable.

Some children are very sensitive to the medication's adverse effect on sleep and/or appetite and it may be best to opt for a shorter duration of action to enable the child to eat between doses and to ensure that the effect of the medicine has worn off by the evening mealtime and by bedtime.

It is not advisable to start a child on a long-acting preparation when the medicine is taken for the first time. First, it is important to ensure that a longer duration of action is really necessary by experimenting with the short-acting form by adding doses sequentially through the day if required. Second, as any potential adverse effect of the medication is likely to be more marked when the medication is first introduced, it is better that such a problem be as short-lived as possible.

It is therefore best to start a child on the short-acting form and to change to a long-acting form once the child's response to the medication and the optimal daily dose have been determined.

Some long-acting preparations, such as 'Concerta', are capsules that have to be swallowed whole and so children who are unable to swallow capsules cannot take these. There are some long-acting methylphenidate preparations, such as Ritalin LA and Metadate CD, where the capsule can be opened and the contents sprinkled onto a fluid or semi-solid food (such as juice, honey, or yogurt) so swallowing difficulties should not be a problem.

Although long-acting preparations are manufactured in different strengths, they cannot be divided into smaller doses. Even if a capsule can be opened, *all* of the contents must be swallowed. The beads inside the capsule cannot be subdivided, as the proportions of immediate- and delayed-release beads present in the capsule will then be altered. So for those children who require very small doses of medication, long-acting medication may not be available in a small enough dose.

Types of long-acting preparation

The first long-acting preparations developed in the 1980s were unreliably absorbed and not widely used. Although available in the USA, they did not meet the safety criteria of some other countries, such as the UK and Australia. The active medication was often not absorbed from the capsule. Sometimes the whole contents of a capsule would be absorbed at the same time (dumping). Either way the therapeutic action was unpredictable and there were concerns about safety.

In the 1990s, more sophisticated methods of manufacturing long-acting preparations were developed and these 'second generation' long-acting preparations are safe and reliable.

First generation preparations include Ritalin-SR, dexamphetamine spansules, and compounded sustained-release capsules manufactured by pharmacists. The latter are made by crushing the methyl-phenidate or dexamphetamine tablets and blending them with methylcellulose gel (a form of plant fiber). These preparations should not be used, as the second-generation forms have superseded them.

Second generation long-acting preparations are of two types: capsules that act as micropumps (e.g. Concerta) and capsules that contain a mixture of immediate- and delayed-release beads (e.g. Ritalin LA, Adderall XR, and Metadate-CD).

'Micro-pump' capsules (e.g. Concerta)   These are capsules that, once swallowed, act as tiny methyl-phenidate pumps. An example of this form of medication is 'Concerta'.

The methylphenidate in a Concerta capsule is in the form of a compound known as a polymer. The polymer is of a thicker consistency than the ordinary form of methylphenidate. The casing of a Concerta capsule is lined by a special membrane that allows fluid normally present in the stomach and intestine to pass into the capsule, but does not allow the methylphenidate-polymer to pass out of the capsule. The only way the polymer can escape from inside the capsule is through a tiny laser-drilled hole ('exit port') at one end of the capsule. This port is so narrow, and the polymer so thick, that the methylphenidate can only escape if actively pushed from inside the capsule. This is achieved by a compartment within the capsule known as the 'push-compartment'. When a Concerta capsule is swallowed, fluid in the stomach and intestines is absorbed through the capsule wall and enters the push-compartment causing it to swell gradually. The push-compartment is situated at the opposite end of the capsule from the exit port and as it swells, it squeezes the methyl-phenidate through the exit port and into the intestines where it is absorbed.

The steady flow of methylphenidate from the exit port of a Concerta capsule is too gradual to initiate the effect of the methylphenidate. For this reason the Concerta capsule is also coated with a layer of non-polymerized methylphenidate that is rapidly absorbed shortly after the capsule is swallowed. This produces a burst of methylphenidate that raises the amount of methylphenidate in the bloodstream to a therapeutic level. This level is then maintained by the steady stream of methylphenidate extruded through the exit port. The total duration of action of a Concerta capsule is approximately 9 hours.

Concerta capsules are so tough that they can only be cracked open with a mallet. They cannot be digested and so pass intact through the intestines. The difficulty extracting the methylphenidate from the capsule and the unsuitability of the polymer for sniffing (snorting) or injecting (mainlining) make it almost impossible to abuse.

Timed-release beads in a capsule   Examples of this form of long-acting preparation are 'Ritalin LA' (not to be confused with the ordinary 'Ritalin' tablets, or the superceded Ritalin SR), 'Adderall XR' capsules (not to be confused with the ordinary 'Adderall' tablets), and 'Metadate-CD'.

Ritalin LA, Adderall XR, and Metadate-CD capsules contain a mixture of two types of beads. Half of the beads are released immediately after the capsule is swallowed. The release of the medicine in the other half of the beads is delayed for approximately 4 hours. The medication is therefore absorbed in two separate 'pulses' or 'phases' (biphasic release). This doubles the duration of action of the medicine. Taking a 20 mg capsule of Ritalin LA would be the equivalent of taking 10 mg of standard Ritalin followed by another 10 mg of standard Ritalin 4 hours later.

Other forms of stimulant medication

Single-isomer methylphenidate (Focalin)

The common brands of methylphenidate, such as Ritalin, consist of a mixture of equal quantities of two different forms of methylphenidate molecules. These forms, known as 'isomers', are mirror images of one another. They can be thought of as the two forms of the human hand, the right-hand and the left-hand. The two hands are analogous, but differently orientated in space. The 'right-handed' molecules of methylphenidate are the 'dextro isomer' (*dextro* is the Greek word for 'right') and the left-handed molecules are the 'levo isomer' (*levo* is the Greek word for 'left').

Only the dextro isomer has therapeutic properties. The levo isomer has no therapeutic effect but, unfortunately, it possesses the same side effects as the dextro isomer.

It is for this reason that a pure dextro isomer has been manufactured and marketed. It has the trade name 'Focalin'.

Since all the methylphenidate in a Focalin tablet is therapeutically active, only half the amount of methylphenidate by weight has to be given. For example, 5 mg of Focalin is equivalent to 10 mg of Ritalin in its therapeutic potency. The advantage of Focalin is that the absence of the undesirable levo isomer reduces the frequency and severity of any side effects by 50%.

Mixed salts of dexamphetamine (Adderall)

The standard form of dexamphetamine used to treat ADHD is the sulphate salt (dexamphetamine sulphate). When we refer to 'dexamphetamine tablets' we mean tablets containing this single salt.

Tablets containing a mixture of two salts of dexamphetamine together with two salts of amphetamine have been marketed under the trade name 'Adderall' since 1996. The four salts in an Adderall tablet are: dexamphetamine sulphate, dexamphetamine saccharate, amphetamine aspartate-monohydrate, and amphetamine sulphate. Each one of these salts makes up a quarter of the tablet by weight.

Adderall may be preferable to pure dexamphetamine sulphate in some children. Its potential advantages are as follows:

- *Intermediate duration of action* The saccharate and aspartate salts are longer acting than the sulphate, extending the action from approximately 5 hours for a standard dexamphetamine sulphate tablet, to approximately 7 hours for Adderall. This is not long enough to be considered 'long-acting', but is intermediate between short and long-acting. This intermediate duration of action may be sufficient to make an in-school dose unnecessary for some children.

- *Dose flexibility* While Adderall cannot match the long-acting medicines for duration of action, it has one attribute that long-acting medicines do not possess—its duration of action is retained even when the tablet is broken into pieces. This is because its longer action relates to its ingredients not its physical properties. To take advantage of this, Adderall tablets are double-scored so that they can be more accurately divided into quarters. In children who require a slightly longer duration of action, but need a very small dose of medication, Adderall may be the appropriate choice.

- *Smooth onset of action* The four different salts in Adderall do not start working at the same time. This gives Adderall a gradual onset of action spread over time. This may be advantageous in children who experience a sense of 'nervousness', or a 'shaky' feeling, when standard dexamphetamine sulphate tablets 'kick in' suddenly.

- *Smooth drop-off of action* Even more useful than the gentle onset of action with Adderall, is its slow and smooth drop-off in action as the different salts wear off one by one. This may eradicate the 'rebound' moodiness that occurs in some children when the effect of a standard dexamphetamine sulphate tablet drops off suddenly.

Generic brands of methylphenidate

When a chemical compound is marketed as a medicine for the first time, it is given a brand name by the company that first developed and patented it. This is referred to as the 'original-brand'. For the next 20 years, only that company—the holder of the patent—can produce the chemical compound for sale. Some drugs have several patents that may prolong the exclusivity period beyond 20 years.

When the patent eventually expires, other companies are allowed to market the chemical compound. These companies cannot use the original-brand name, they must market their version under either its chemical (generic) name or a brand name of their own. It is these, non-original brands, that are referred to as 'generic drugs' (or generic-brands) to distinguish them from the original-brand.

When the chemical compound, methylphenidate, was first developed by the pharmaceutical company, Ciba-Geigy, it was given the brand name 'Ritalin'. For many years Ritalin was the only brand of methylphenidate available. The name Ritalin remained unchanged when ownership of Ciba-Geigy passed to Novartis[*] after a company takeover.

Now that the patent for methylphenidate has expired, generic brands of methylphenidate have appeared on the market. They contain the same active ingredient but have different names[†].

In most countries, the manufacturer of the generic drug is not required to duplicate the original medical studies when applying for approval by the registering body. The only requirement is that the generic drug be shown to be equivalent to the original.

Some doctors are satisfied that generic drugs are no less effective than the original-brand; others are concerned that subtle differences in absorption and therapeutic effectiveness may exist. They point to differences in manufacturing processes and in the inactive 'fillers' that are added in the manufacture of tablets. If doubt exists, it is best to stick to the original-brand whenever possible.

Non-stimulant medications

Tofranil (Imipramine)

Tofranil has been used for many years to treat bedwetting in children, as well as to treat depression in both children and adults. Its usefulness in children with ADHD has been well established.

---

[*]*In the UK only, the pharmaceutical company, Cephalon, is the exclusive marketer of Ritalin under an agreement with Novartis.*
[†]*Examples of generic brand names for methylphenidate are 'Equasym' (UK), 'Methylin' (USA), and 'Attenta' (Australia).*

It is used in smaller doses in children with ADHD than for bedwetting and depression. However, in children with ADHD who have bedwetting or depression in addition to ADHD, larger doses can be taken.

Tofranil is a long-acting medicine that remains in the body for some 8 hours after a tablet is taken. The medicine is given regularly with the aim of achieving a steady level in the blood. For this reason, the exact timing of each dose is not as critical as it is for Ritalin and dexamphetamine.

Because the blood level must be built up slowly, it usually takes 2 weeks before the full action of Tofranil becomes evident.

Tofranil will help with all the major difficulties seen in children with ADHD. It improves concentration, decreases impulsivity, and reduces oppositional behavior.

Dosage and administration

The aim of treatment with Tofranil is to achieve a steady level in the blood and consequently the medicine is given 7 days a week. The first tablet is given with breakfast, the second can be given at lunchtime, or on return from school. Sometimes a third tablet is given in the evening as well. The medicine is available in two sizes: 10 mg and 25 mg tablets.

Side effects

Tofranil is used in such low doses for ADHD that side effects are uncommon. When treatment is first started, the child may suffer from sleepiness or easy fatigability, but these are usually mild and resolve after a week or two.

Other possible side effects are slight dryness of the mouth, constipation, and excessive perspiration. It is very rare for these side effects to be trouble-some enough to necessitate stopping the medicine. Constipation can usually be counteracted by ensuring that the child has sufficient dietary fiber.

The occasional child will have a decrease in appetite on Tofranil, but this is rarely as prominent as with Ritalin or dexamphetamine.

One of the drawbacks of Tofranil is that the positive effects may wear off over time. This is known as the development of 'tolerance', and may be remedied by raising the dose, or stopping the medicine for a period before re-introducing it.

Tofranil should not be used in children with disorders of heart rhythm. Such disorders are rare, but it is best for the doctor to arrange for the child's electrocardiograph (electrical trace of heart rhythm) to be checked prior to commencing treatment.

Withdrawal

When the Tofranil is no longer needed, it is usual to withdraw it gradually over a couple of weeks in order to prevent 'rebound depression'. This is not necessary if the dose taken is only 10 mg a day.

Clonidine (Catapres, Dixirit)

In the late 1970s it was first proposed that clonidine, a medicine that had been used for a decade to prevent migraines and treat high blood pressure, might be effective in treating ADHD. This has now been well established.

The main effect of clonidine is on the neurotransmitter norepinephrine and it is extremely effective in children with oppositional or aggressive behavior. It can also reduce anxiety. Sometimes clonidine is taken in the evening only to promote sleep in children with ADHD who suffer from insomnia.

Clonidine combines well with either Ritalin or dexamphetamine, and children can be treated with combinations of clonidine and one of these two medicines. Often the effect of clonidine in combination with these medicines results in better control of the ADHD, as well as a reduction in side effects. This is because clonidine counteracts one of the main side effects of Ritalin and dexamphetamine: insomnia. Clonidine promotes sleep and so it often cures the insomnia caused by Ritalin or dexamphetamine.

Clonidine has a greater effect on behavior, particularly aggression, temper tantrums, and defiance, than it does on concentration. For this reason the combination with Ritalin or dexamphetamine (both of whose primary action is on concentration) is complementary.

For daytime symptoms

When it is used for daytime symptoms of ADHD, clonidine must be given regularly in order to achieve a constant level in the bloodstream. It is given at least twice a day, and in some children up to 4 times a day, in order to achieve a steady level in the blood. Clonidine must be taken 7 days a week. When treatment is commenced, the improvement may not be evident for several weeks. The earliest effect is usually observed after 10 days, but it may take 2 or 3 months before the maximal beneficial effect is apparent.

For insomnia

Children with ADHD often have great difficulty falling asleep. Their minds are so active that even young children with the disorder may remain awake until the early hours of the morning. Many children with the condition become very distressed by their inability to fall asleep, which only makes this difficulty worse. Many are exhausted and irritable the next day because of lack of sleep.

The first step in helping such a child should always be by non-medical means. The child should not have any stimulating food or drink (such as tea, coffee, cola, or chocolate) before bedtime. He should not be allowed to play computer games, watch violent TV shows or videos, or listen to stimulating music (such as 'techno' music) before bed. Arguments and schoolwork should also be avoided late in the evening if possible. Soothing background music, calming stories, or meditations may be helpful at bedtime. Warm milk drinks may also help some children to settle at night.

If the insomnia remains a significant problem despite these measures, a small dose of clonidine at night may be helpful. Clonidine is far preferable to sleeping tablets because it is not habit-forming. It does not make the child sleepy, but settles his mind so that he can relax. The effect comes on after approximately 1 hour and is short-lived so the child should try to sleep during the first couple of hours after it has started to work.

When it is used to promote sleep in children with ADHD, clonidine is given as a single evening dose 1 hour prior to bedtime. At first a small dose is tried and this is gradually increased until the desired effect is attained or the maximal permissible dose is reached.

The medication does not have to be given every night. It can be reserved for nights when non-medical measures to promote sleep have failed.

Dosage and administration

Clonidine is sometimes available in a small, coated tablet (Dixirit) marketed to prevent migraine, and a larger uncoated tablet (Catapres) used to treat high blood pressure. Either of these preparations can be used, but Catapres tablets will need to be broken into quarters or halves for most children with ADHD.

In some countries, clonidine is also available in the form of a skin patch, which is a small bandage impregnated with the medicine that adheres to the skin (usually on the back). The medicine is then absorbed steadily through the skin during the day. This avoids the necessity for repeated tablet taking for a child who takes it to control daytime symptoms. The only problem is that the child may pull off the skin patch.

Side effects

Clonidine is free of any significant side effects when used in the doses usually required for ADHD. Some children may become drowsy when they first start this medicine, but this side effect quickly subsides.

Clonidine is usually used in such small doses in ADHD that there is no appreciable effect on blood pressure. Some children may feel dizzy if the dose is excessive, and this may indicate that their blood pressure is being lowered. The dose should then be reduced.

Parents should be aware that behavior *may initially deteriorate* when treatment with clonidine commences. If treatment is continued, the positive effects will be seen after 2 or 3 weeks. Parents may therefore have to prepare for some worsening of behavior when treatment with clonidine is started.

For children who have migraines in addition to ADHD, treatment with clonidine may prevent their headaches, as clonidine is also used in small doses to treat migraine. Ironically, despite its use to treat migraine, clonidine can *cause* headaches in some children.

Withdrawal

When clonidine is used for daytime symptoms of ADHD and treatment involves the use of more than 50 µg of clonidine a day, the medicine should not be stopped suddenly. It should be withdrawn slowly over a period of 2 to 3 weeks to prevent 'rebound hypertension', a condition where blood pressure rises on sudden cessation of clonidine.

When a child is taking a dose above 50 µg a day, he should not miss a dose for the same reason. However, even if a dose is missed, it is extremely unlikely that any harm will ensue.

If treatment involves less than 50 µg per day, clonidine can be stopped abruptly when no longer needed.

When clonidine is taken as a single nightly dose to promote sleep, withdrawal is not a problem regardless of the dose taken.

Aurorix (moclobemide)

The destruction of the neurotransmitters dopamine and norepinephrine in nerve cells involves an enzyme known as a monoamine oxidase.

The action of this enzyme can be counteracted by medicines known as monoamine oxidase inhibitors (MAO-I). Their effect is to increase the amount of these neurotransmitters in the synapse.

MOA inhibitors have been used for a long time to treat depression. However, they have always had the disadvantage that people taking such a medicine had to be careful not to eat certain foods (such as cheese) because of the risk of dangerous interactions. This made the use of MOA inhibitors in children with ADHD fraught with difficulties.

A second generation of MOA inhibitors are available that are reversible, and do not require any dietary restrictions. One of these, moclobemide (Aurorix), is effective in treating some children with ADHD.

Dose and administration

Moclobemide is usually given in a dose of 75 mg twice a day (i.e. half a tablet twice a day). Increasing the dose does not result in a better response. However, the dose may be increased if a child has depression in association with ADHD, so that the moclobemide can treat the depression as well.

The medicine is given 7 days a week, and it usually takes 1 or 2 weeks before the effect is apparent. When the medicine is no longer needed, it is best to withdraw it slowly.

The child can remain on his usual diet while taking this medicine.

Side effects

Moclobemide is very free of side effects. Difficulties with falling asleep and a decrease in appetite may occur, but are rare.

Risperidone (Risperdal)

Risperidone can be an extremely effective medicine in children with ADHD. It is used mainly for children in whom oppositional and aggressive behavior is a major problem. However, it may have an adverse effect on learning so all children taking this medicine for ADHD should have their academic attainments carefully monitored.

Risperidone is a long-acting medicine and must be given on a regular basis to achieve a therapeutic response. It should be given 7 days a week. It usually takes 2 weeks before the full effect is seen.

Risperidone mainly works by blocking dopamine autoreceptors at the synapse.

A drawback of risperidone is that it is an expensive medicine.

Side effects

Risperidone may cause sleepiness but this usually subsides after a few days.

It may increase appetite, which can be a problem in children who experience an excessive weight gain on this medicine.

Risperidone increases the sensitivity of the skin to sunburn, so sunscreens should be used when the child is exposed to the sun.

Risperidone belongs to a group of medicines known as 'phenothiazines'. Any phenothiazine may cause abnormal movements if given in high doses for extended periods. Occasionally, these abnormal movements may persist even when the medicine is ceased. These abnormal movements are referred to as 'tardive dyskinesia'. The word, 'tardive', means late, indicating that the disorder takes time to develop. The prefix, 'dys', signifies abnormal and 'kinesia' is the Greek word for movement. So a tardive dyskinesia is a series of abnormal movements occurring late in a course of treatment with a phenothiazine.

Tardive dyskinesias usually involve the face and mouth (e.g. poking out of the tongue and blowing out of the cheeks). These movements may be accompanied by movements of hands or feet (e.g. 'piano playing' movements of the fingers and foot tapping). The dyskinesias may be occasional or continuous, hardly noticeable, or very obvious. Mild symptoms may not initially be noticed by the child or his parents.

While risperidone has a considerably lower risk of this side effect than other phenothiazines, and although children are less likely to develop tardive dyskinesias than adults, all children treated with this medication should be monitored for this potentially irreversible side effect.

If a child taking risperidone develops unusual movements, his doctor should be consulted as soon as possible. In most cases the medication will need to be withdrawn.

Risperidone should only be used if no other medicine for ADHD is suitable. It should always be given in the smallest effective dose and should not be continued for longer than is necessary.

Despite these concerns, risperidone can play a very important role in helping some children with ADHD when no other medicine is effective. Used conservatively and with proper monitoring, this medicine can be taken for several years with no adverse effects. Although the risk of tardive dyskinesia must be considered, it should be noted that this side effect has not yet been described after treatment with risperidone.

Atomoxetine (Strattera)

A new mediation, atomoxetine (Strattera), which was developed by the pharmaceutical company Eli Lilly, was released in the USA in early 2003.

Atomoxetine is neither a stimulant nor an amphetamine. Its action is not on dopamine, but on another neurotransmitter, norepinephrine, that is involved in some cases of ADHD. Atomoxetine selectively inhibits the re-uptake of norepinephrine by the nerve that produced it, thereby making more norepinephrine available for transmission of the impulse. This mode of action means that atomoxetine may be useful for some children with ADHD who do not respond to stimulant medication.

Atomoxetine is a long-acting medicine and a single morning dose will last into the evening. It does not cause difficulty falling asleep and can therefore be used to help children who have difficulties in the late afternoon and evening. It is also useful for children who have difficulties in the early morning as it is present in the body on waking.

The release of this new, non-amphetamine medication for ADHD has caused much excitement in the media and among parents. It may be favored over stimulants by some parents because of the adverse publicity given to Ritalin by the media. Nevertheless, it should be remembered that atomoxetine is a new medicine, without a long-term safety record. The stimulants, by contrast, have been used for over 65 years and have a well-established record of long-term safety.

Section 6

17

Unconventional treatments

The treatment of ADHD outlined in this book involves the combination of a number of different modes of treatment (multi-modal treatment) selected according to the needs of the individual child. These treatments include behavior modification programs, remedial education, and medication. Such treatments must be individualized and kept under regular review so that they can be modified, as the child's needs change. Scientifically conducted trials have shown that this form of multimodal treatment provides the best results over time.

Evaluating an alternative treatment

There are no quick and easy ways of overcoming ADHD and no outright cures. Unfortunately many misguided or dishonest individuals promote all manner of alternative 'treatments' for ADHD. Such treatments may be claimed to cure the condition or ameliorate symptoms.

Some alternative treatments are a waste of time and money that could be spent more profitably in other ways to benefit the child. Some are potentially harmful to the physical and/or psychological well-being of the child. Some may have detrimental effects on the family as a whole.

It is important, therefore, that you obtain reliable information from your child's doctor before becoming involved in any treatment. Do not rely on stories of miraculous cures from those who promote or have used these treatments. Children with ADHD generally show improvement over time. In addition, almost any intervention will have a positive effect because the mere act of doing something for the child will raise her morale and boost her self-esteem. Changes should not be ascribed to a particular treatment without independent scientific evaluation.

Evaluations should be by controlled trials published in reputable scientific journals. Such trials should be carried out 'blind', meaning that the person who assessed the performance of children both on and off the treatment did not know which had received the treatment and which had not until after the assessments were completed. If the treatment consists of a medicine, the untreated group should have received a dummy medicine (placebo) to make the comparison valid. In addition, the person who carried out the trial should not have had a vested interest in the treatment.

An increasing number of independent trials of controversial treatments are now reported in scientific journals. In addition, professional and government bodies often make policy statements about certain treatments based on reviews of the scientific data.

If you plan to start a treatment, first be certain that you understand the risks involved. Decide upon what outcome you wish to see, and how long it should take before this occurs. If the objective improvement is not achieved, treatment should cease. Do not allow yourself to accept some vague improvements decided upon at a later date.

The role of the media

The media (television, newspaper, and radio) often play an active role in promoting controversial treatments. Journalists and reporters are continually on the lookout for attention-grabbing stories that will increase their circulation or ratings. Unfortunately, many journalists and reporters covering medical matters have little, if any, scientific training. Some are prepared to quote selectively in order to make their coverage more interesting.

Producers of radio and television programs, particularly those dealing with current affairs and health matters, are aware that sensationalism improves ratings. They may therefore cover alternative treatments with an eye to entertainment rather than to providing balanced information. A common tendency is to promote a treatment as novel (therefore justifying its coverage and creating excitement and interest) even when it has been available for some time and has been shown to be ineffective.

Unscrupulous media presenters are greatly assisted in their efforts by the desire for publicity of those who provide these treatments. By contrast, many conventional experts avoid media appearances because of concern that they may be accused of advertizing or self-promotion by their professional regulatory bodies and colleagues.

Parents should therefore be very wary of media coverage of ADHD. This also applies to information about treatment of ADHD on the internet, as many sites that purport to provide balanced information have been established to promote a particular form of treatment. The accuracy of information on the internet is not subjected to any test of validity or authenticity. A list of reputable internet sites dealing with ADHD is listed in the Appendix of this book.

Some widely promoted treatments

Although numerous controversial treatments are promoted, with new ones continually developed, most fall into one of a number of categories. These are: dietary treatments, herbal treatments, programs involving technological apparatus, exercises, manipulations, and meditation.

Dietary treatments

Dietary treatments for ADHD are based on beliefs about the ways in which food may play a role in causing or aggravating ADHD. The mechanisms suggested are food intolerance, food allergy, and dietary deficiency.

Food intolerance occurs when the body lacks substances required to digest or metabolize food, with the resultant accumulation of harmful substances derived from the incomplete digestion or faulty metabolism of the food by the body.

Allergy occurs when a specific part of the body's immune system interacts with a component of food to generate a harmful reaction.

Dietary deficiency occurs when the diet is lacking in a particular component required for maintaining health.

Removing the harmful substance from the diet (an elimination diet) treats intolerance and allergy, while administering the deficient substance as a dietary supplement corrects deficiency. Both elimination diets and dietary supplements have been promoted as treatments for ADHD.

Elimination diets

Exclusion diets are based on two commonly held beliefs: first, that ADHD is a new condition related to the modern life-style and, second, that food allergy is a common cause of behavioral problems in children. The validity of these beliefs needs to be examined.

Is ADHD a modern condition?

ADHD was first described in the medical literature over 100 years ago and there are numerous accounts of children with similar problems in general literature extending back to medieval times.

Unfortunately, ADHD was often not recognized in the past. Even as recently as 20 years ago, children with ADHD were often severely punished at school because of their learning and behavioral difficulties. Many of these children left school early without acquiring basic academic skills. Many adults recall children in their class at school who fitted the description of ADHD but were not given the benefit of having their condition diagnosed and treated. With the greater demand for educational qualifications in the employment market, parents are now far more likely to seek assistance for a child with educational and/or behavioral difficulties. The resultant increase in diagnosis of ADHD has led to the widespread misconception that it is a new phenomenon.

Is food allergy a factor in ADHD?

There is no doubt that allergic disorders, such as asthma and hay-fever, may impair a child's ability to concentrate and to behave appropriately because they undermine a sufferer's feeling of well-being. Such clear-cut allergic disorders may therefore worsen the condition of a child with co-existing ADHD and should be properly treated. However, the belief that ADHD itself is caused by food allergy in the absence of such specific conditions, as is suggested in some quarters, is unsupported by research findings. Those who make such claims have not produced satisfactory evidence to support their assertions. On the contrary, the evidence that ADHD is due to a genetic impairment in neurotransmitter metabolism, (see Chapter 10) is incontrovertible.

The practice of putting children with ADHD on allergy diets to improve concentration or behavior is not justified in the light of the scientific evidence. Blood and skin tests for allergy have no place in the treatment of ADHD. They are not even reliable indicators in true allergic conditions.

Pitfalls of elimination diets

Elimination diets often appeal to parents because they allow them to gain control over at least one aspect of the child's life: her food intake. Unfortunately this can lead to a great deal of conflict with the child.

Many children with ADHD are in continual conflict with their parents over many issues and adding another one should be avoided unless necessary.

Dietary control is easiest when the child is young and parents are in control of what she eats—as the child grows older she may become less willing to keep to the diet and may surreptitiously eat forbidden foods. She will usually resent her parents' attempts to control her and she will want to eat the same foods as her peers.

If a child is put on an exclusion diet, it should be supervised by a doctor to ensure that she is receiving adequate nutrition. Radical exclusion diets, in which one or more food groups are excluded, may be dangerous and should be avoided.

The best way to evaluate the diet is for an independent observer, such as a teacher, to monitor the child's performance without knowing when she is on the diet and when she is eating normally. It is important that the observation extends over three periods: when the child is on a normal diet, when she is on the elimination diet, and then when she is back on the normal diet. If the diet is truly helping the child, her condition should improve on the elimination diet *and* deteriorate again when the normal diet is commenced

Some examples of exclusion diets

The Feingold diet

In 1973 a Californian allergist, Dr Benjamin Feingold, published a book, 'Why Your Child Is Hyperactive'. In his book, Dr Feingold proposed that certain substances in the diet were the cause of hyperactivity in children. Despite the fact that Dr Feingold's theory was not based on scientific research, it was extensively covered by the media and came to be widely accepted by large sections of the general population.

The supposedly harmful dietary substances identified by Dr Feingold were artificial colorings, flavorings, and preservatives added to food. He also implicated a group of substances known as salicylates, some of which occur naturally in some foods. To treat hyperactivity, he proposed what is now known as the 'Feingold diet'. This diet excludes all foods containing the substances implicated by Feingold. Many fruits are not permitted in the diet as they contain naturally occurring salicylates. As preservatives, colorings, and flavorings are ubiquitous in food, the diet is very restrictive and involves a major change in shopping, cooking, and eating. Dr Feingold also recommended the avoidance of over-the-counter and prescription medicines as well as certain other substances such as toothpastes, mouthwashes, and perfumes.

Current recommendations advocated by followers of Dr Feingold involve a two-stage plan that begins with elimination of artificial colors and flavors, certain antioxidants (BHA, BHT, and TBHQ), and salicylate-containing products (including foods containing naturally occurring salicylates). If improvement occurs and lasts for over 4 weeks, the proscribed foods are then reintroduced one at a time to check if they can be tolerated.

Many parents who have followed Feingold's recommendations have reported improvement in their child's behavior. However, carefully designed experiments have generally failed to support the idea that the diet results in the improvements claimed by its supporters. When improvements have occurred, they affected a small minority of children, were small, and were short-lived.

The diet is of no benefit in children with the predominantly inattentive form of ADHD, but may cause some slight improvement in the overactivity, impulsivity, task persistence, and distractibility of a small proportion of children with the hyperactive-impulsive and combined forms of the condition.

The diet is difficult to keep to in its strict form but is nutritionally sound, provided care is taken to ensure that there is an adequate intake of vitamin C.

Experts have noted inconsistencies in Feingold's 1975 book. The foods he recommended include some that are high in salicylates and exclude others that are low in salicylates.

Sugar-free diets

Sugar and aspartame (an artificial sweetener) have been blamed for hyperactivity, but well-designed studies have found no evidence supporting such claims.

Gluten-free diet

Gluten is a protein found in wheat, rye, and oats. The only condition to be associated with gluten intolerance is celiac disease, a condition unrelated to ADHD. The diagnosis of celiac disease should only be made by a gastroenterologist (a specialist in the stomach and intestines).

Diary-free diet

Allergy to cow's milk protein may cause symptoms such as rash and wheezing, while milk-sugar (lactose) intolerance may cause abdominal discomfort and diarrhoea. Neither of these conditions plays a role in the causation of ADHD.

Dietary supplementation

While it is true that brain neurotransmitters are formed from certain elements in our diet, ADHD is due to a genetically determined defect in neurotransmitter metabolism at the synapse that is unrelated to nutritional components of neurotransmitter formation.

In the Western diet there are excess amounts of all the substances (substrates) required for neurotransmitter production, and nutritional deficiencies leading to ADHD have never been described.

Examples of dietary supplements

Numerous trials of supplements in children with ADHD have been reported in the medical literature. Substances studied have included, amino-acid mixtures, essential fatty acids (e.g. fish oil), L-carnitine, glyconutritional supplements, dimethylaminoethano, mega-vitamin mixtures, and minerals (iron, zinc, and magnesium).

None of these substances has been shown to be of a benefit to children with ADHD. Some may be detrimental to a child's health. For example, excessive amounts of fat-soluble vitamins (vitamins A and D) cannot be readily excreted by the body and may accumulate and cause toxic effects, slowing down the child's development, and causing ill-health and even death.

High doses of vitamins (mega-vitamins) and minerals are often advocated by those calling themselves 'orthomolecular physicians'. Such practitioners often analyze a child's hair and blood to obtain a 'profile' of vitamin and mineral 'deficiencies'. The levels regarded as abnormal by many of these physicians are usually considered to be within the normal range by conventional doctors.

'Efalex' is a patented combination of a fish (tuna) oil supplement, a herbal extract (evening primrose oil), and mega-vitamin (vitamin E). It has been very actively marketed as a treatment for a number of conditions including ADHD. Its originator and patent-holder, Jacqueline Stordy, has traveled the word giving talks to encourage its sales and has written a book to promote its use.

An objective examination of the reports used to back up its use shows no scientific evidence of any benefits to children with ADHD.

The large amount of vitamin E in the product raises concern about its long-term safety in children. Vitamin E is a fat-soluble vitamin that cannot be excreted by the child's body when present in excessive amounts. The high fat content of the preparation may also interfere with absorption of medications taken concurrently for treatment of ADHD and so render them less effective.

Herbal treatments

There has been a proliferation of herbal substances promoted for the treatment of ADHD. These include Ginko biloba, evening primrose flower, St John's wort (hypericum), Brahmi herbs (Bacopa monniera and Centella asiatica), pycnogenol (extracted from pine bark or grape seeds), and a range of Chinese herbal cocktails.

Such substances are promoted on the basis that they are a 'natural' form of treatment. This claim is often accepted at face value without careful consideration of its validity or implications. A number of fundamental questions should be considered before accepting the concept that 'natural is best'.

First, is the *treatment*, and not just the *substance* used, in fact 'natural'? Second, are natural substances necessarily safe? Third, are natural substances adequately tested for efficacy and safety?

Is the treatment in fact 'natural'?

The fact that a treatment involves a naturally occurring substance does not make the treatment itself 'natural'. For example, if a child is given a naturally occurring substance that is not part of the normal human diet, such as the oil extracted from the evening primrose plant, this cannot be regarded as a 'natural' treatment. The plant may have produced the oil naturally, but it is not natural for a child to ingest large amounts of this oil on a regular basis. Children do not normally eat evening primroses and, even if they did, they could never ingest enough to take in the amount of oil present in the extract. Administering such an extract to child must be regarded as unnatural and experimental. There is a risk that the ingestion of this oil may be harmful to the child. This raises the second question.

Are naturally occurring substances necessarily safe?

The answer to this question should be obvious. One has only to consider such naturally occurring plants such as the tobacco plant, the deadly nightshade, the opium poppy, or the cannabis plant to realize that nature is full of harmful substances. Every year many individuals are hospitalized because of the toxic effects of plants. Some of these individuals succumb to the effects of these plants on organs such as the liver and kidneys. Some of the most beautiful plants with the most alluring names are among the most toxic, a phenomenon that has been referred to as 'the siren syndrome'. A pretty flower on the label of a bottle of herbal treatment is no guarantee of the safety of its contents. This raises the third question.

Are artificial substances adequately tested for efficacy and safety?

Many drugs prescribed by conventional doctors are extracted from plants and other living organisms. For example, the drug *digitalis* comes from the foxglove, *penicillin* from potato mould, and *vincristine* from the periwinkle flower.

Before such plant extracts can be sold as conventional medicines, they have to be subjected to rigorous checks of purity and numerous clinical trials of efficacy and safety. They must then be registered for use by a government authority that will place controls on standards of manufacture, availability, and the content of prescribing information available to doctors and consumers. All adverse effects must be reported by doctors and pharmacists to a government monitoring body. When they are prescribed, very precise doses are prescribed and dispensed, based on scientifically conducted research.

Naturally occurring substances used by alternative practitioners are not subjected to the same checks and evaluations. Their manufacture is often crude and haphazard and their use based on anecdote and faith rather than on scientific evidence. Toxic effects become apparent only through usage and may not be reported. Only now, for example, are we discovering the side effects of alternative medicines such as St John's wort and Valerian. They have been accepted as 'safe' for many years without having undergone the rigorous evaluation to which all medicinal substance should be routinely subjected before use.

When many herbal substances used as treatments have been subjected to controlled trials, beneficial effects were not found.

Technological treatments

Treatments that involve the use of some form of special electronic equipment often impress parents and their children. However, no matter how sophisticated the technology, claims made for such treatments should be subjected to the same scientific testing of efficacy and safety as any other mode of treatment.

The main examples of such treatments are EEG biofeedback therapy (neurotherapy) and sound therapy (SAMONAS and Tomatis methods).

EEG biofeedback therapy

In this form of treatment, sometimes known as neurotherapy, the child's brain wave pattern (EEG) is monitored while she is trained to increase certain frequencies of brain electrical activity. To monitor the EEG, the child wears a cap on her head onto which wires are attached. These wires are connected to a computer that continuously measures brain electricity during the training session. The software on the computer enables the child to play computer games that reward her if she is able to alter her brain wave pattern in the way desired. Claims are made that such training sessions decrease the symptoms of ADHD.

Proponents of the treatment consider that a child needs at least 80 sessions. Each session last approximately 30 minutes.

EEG biofeedback is not new: it has been used for over 30 years; however, the decreasing cost of computers and the fact that a license is not required to carry out EEG-biofeedback, means that such treatments are now more widely available and are actively marketed.

After three decades of use, despite claims to the contrary by those who have a vested interest in the treatment, there is no scientific evidence for the efficacy of EEG-biofeedback in the treatment of children with ADHD.

Sound therapy

In this treatment, the child listens to specially prepared recorded music (on cassette or compact disc). The recordings have been electronically modified to remove or introduce specific sound frequencies. These modifications are not audible to the listener who hears only ordinary (usually classical) music.

The proponents of sound therapy claim the modifications are perceived subliminally and have a positive effect on brain function.

This form of treatment has a great deal of pseudoscience and mystique attached to it. It is sometimes known as the 'Samonas method', an acronym for <u>S</u>pectral <u>A</u>ctivated <u>M</u>usic of <u>O</u>ptimal <u>Na</u>tural <u>S</u>tructure, a description of the way the sound is altered. It is also referred to as the 'Tomatis method' after a Paris ear nose and throat specialist who designed an apparatus called the 'electronic ear' that could manipulate the frequencies of sounds. He claimed that his apparatus could boost deficient sound frequencies heard by a singer so that his or her singing voice would improve. Singers flocked to him for treatment in the 1930s.

Another name attached to sound therapy is that of Patricia Joudry, a Canadian author, who linked up with Benedictine monks in Saskatchewan who had trained in the Tomatis method. She spearheaded the commercialization of the method in the 1980s by selling 'treated' recorded music cassettes for use with portable cassette players which had just come on the market at that time. This 'Joudry method' was promoted in a book written by Patricia and Rafaele Joudry, '*Sound Therapy Music to Recharge your Brain*'. Claims were made that the method cured many conditions including depression, insomnia, chronic fatigue, and hearing loss.

The scientific study of sound therapy is hampered by the fact that there is no consensus among sound therapists about how the sound should be altered. Since the alteration to the sound is not audible, some 'sound therapy' recordings may be ordinary compact discs—any perceived benefit is an example of the 'emperor's new clothes' phenomenon. Properly conducted research has failed to show any significant positive effects of sound therapy for children with ADHD.

Exercise programs

Exercise has been a popular form of alternative treatment for learning and behavioral difficulties in ADHD. Every few years a new program containing variations of the same simple exercises is developed and promoted as a treatment for ADHD.

The media, particularly TV, often give extensive, upbeat coverage of such programs: footage of children carrying out exercise programs provides excellent visual images for TV.

Such treatments usually involve manoeuvres such as getting children to spin, ride a scooter down a ramp, swing, and crawl.

Based on theoretical considerations, and the research evidence, it is highly unlikely that a child can learn a complex skill such as reading or attending to a task by jumping on a trampoline. Time spent on such manoeuvres is probably better utilized giving the child practice at the specific skill that she needs to learn, whether that be spelling or writing neatly.

Examples of exercise programs

Sensori-motor integration

This form of exercise therapy is based on the work of A. Jean Ayres who believed that developmental problems were related to difficulties in processing incoming stimuli. She also believed that the development of higher intellectual processes is dependent on primitive parts of the brain developing first.

The therapy combines exercises and sensory stimulation such as stroking the child's skin with materials of various textures and a battery operated brush.

Ayres claimed that children treated by her methods made exceptional developmental progress; however, independent studies have not confirmed this. In addition to wasting time and resources that could be spent using proven methods of treatment, activities such as spinning and creeping may be humiliating for some children.

DDAT method (Dyslexia, Dyspraxia, and Attention method)

This is the most recent reincarnation of the simplistic belief that a series of exercises can overcome conditions such as reading·disability (dyslexia) and ADHD.

The treatment is a business venture of the UK tycoon, Wynford Dore. He claims the exercises helped his daughter overcome her learning difficulties and has extravagantly promoted his treatment centers with glossy web sites and extensive media publicity. Treatment centers have been established despite the absence of external, longitudinal scientific evidence of any benefit to children with ADHD or dyslexia.

Like all other such exercise programs it has received extensive, positive TV coverage.

The exercises with names such as 'the lizard', 'the octopus, 'commander', 'tortoise', and 'windmills' are similar to t'ai chi exercises. Despite claims to the contrary, the exercises are not new. They bear a marked resemblance to the program of exercises developed over the past 30 years by Dr Harold Levinson from New York. The claims made that children are making spectacular progress, are hard to credit.

Manipulation

Chiropractors use manipulation of the spine as a method of treating all manner of diseases. This form of treatment has not been shown to be of benefit to children with ADHD.

Meditation

The claim has been made that teaching children with ADHD to meditate improves their behavior and learning; however, there is at present no scientific evidence to support this claim.

Section 7

Adulthood

18

Will he grow out of it?

A decade ago the general consensus was that children with ADHD would invariably grow out of their problems. This has now been disproved. In a sizable proportion of children with ADHD, the difficulties persist into adulthood. Such difficulties may take the form of residual ADHD, secondary problems, or a combination of the two.

Residual ADHD

When the difficulties associated with ADHD, such as poor attention span, impulsivity, and restlessness, persist into adult life, this is known as 'residual ADHD' (rADHD).

In the majority of children with ADHD, these difficulties decrease during late adolescence. There may be a gradual decrease between the ages of 12 and 18 years, or it may occur more abruptly (usually around 16–18 years). In some children the improvement in the late teenage years is so marked that their ADHD can be regarded as having completely resolved. This occurs in some 20% of children with ADHD.

In approximately 80% of children with ADHD, the improvement in the teenage years will not be associated with a complete resolution, and approximately 60% will have mild residual ADHD and 20% a severe form. These proportions are shown in Figure 11.

Adults with *mild* residual ADHD will usually not be hampered by their condition. Many will simply 'bypass' their difficulties by making career and other life choices so that their difficulties with sustained attention, social cognition, or impulsivity do not interfere with their day-to-day functioning.

Some adults with this residual form of ADHD may even turn some of their 'difficulties' into advantages. For example, a certain degree of restlessness may help such a person attain goals, because it makes

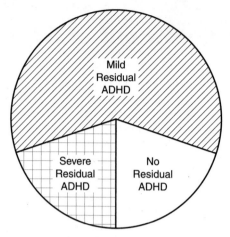

Figure 11 The proportion of children with ADHD who have residual ADHD in adulthood.

him more energetic and less prone to become tired than other people. Impulsivity of thought can also be turned into an advantage if it allows the individual to think laterally and innovatively. Even some minor difficulties with social cognition may allow the individual to be more successful in some endeavors where being forthright is an advantage. Many individuals with mild residual ADHD do extremely well in the business world.

In approximately 20% of children with ADHD, difficulties persist into adulthood in a *severe* form. These individuals have residual ADHD that often hampers their family life and their work. It is these individuals for whom on-going treatment of ADHD during adulthood is essential. This will be discussed later in the chapter.

Secondary problems

The term 'residual ADHD' refers to persistence of the characteristics of ADHD, such as impulsivity and restlessness, into adulthood. Many adults who had ADHD during childhood will have other, secondary, problems that arose *because* of their ADHD in childhood. For example, their ADHD may have resulted in their inability to achieve good academic skills, or may have undermined their self-esteem.

Whether or not the ADHD itself persists, many adults who had ADHD in childhood will continue to suffer as a result of these complications.

Through early treatment of children with ADHD, the secondary problems that ADHD causes during childhood, and which may then persist into adult life, can be diminished or avoided.

It is important to distinguish secondary problems from residual problems. Secondary problems may exist in adults who have residual ADHD, as well as in adults in whom the primary characteristics of ADHD have resolved. The latter group may still need help in the form of counseling, adult education, self-support groups, and specialist help with career advice and employment support.

A person with secondary problems who does *not* have residual ADHD would not benefit from medication for ADHD. This is quite different from adults with residual ADHD, where medication for ADHD may play a very important role in helping ameliorate their symptoms.

Characteristics of residual ADHD

Residual ADHD is due to the persistence of the features of childhood ADHD described in Chapter 1. The characteristics are very similar, but with adulthood the nature of some problems changes.

Adults with ADHD have tremendous difficulty completing projects. They will often have a number of different projects that they are tackling simultaneously without properly following through any of them. Their difficulties with task persistence often involve procrastination; they have great difficulty getting started with a task.

Easy distractibility and difficulties focusing attention are common. Many adults with ADHD complain that they tend to lose track when reading. Their partners and children often complain that they 'tune out' when they speak to them.

Impatience is a very prominent characteristic of residual ADHD. Adults with ADHD are very intolerant of 'red tape'. They have difficulty going through necessary procedures and often develop reputations for being mavericks. They are quick to become frustrated and to give up if they meet adversity.

They are very restless individuals and are intolerant of what they regard as 'boring' activities. They find it very difficult to relax in leisure activities that do not require a high level of activity. They have a low tolerance for frustration and quickly lose their temper or give up if a task requires persistence. They have particular difficulty working at tedious tasks that require incentival motivation (motivation for a reward that is far off in the future).

Adults with ADHD find it difficult to get themselves organized. They can be very creative and intuitive, but will often need someone else to ensure that the more practical, day-to-day arrangements are made.

Impulsivity is a particular problem for adults with residual ADHD. For many, it is the most prominent characteristic. Impulsivity may be seen verbally, in a tendency to say what comes into their mind without necessarily considering the timing or appropriateness of the remark. This may create difficulties in personal and professional interactions. Impulsivity may also be seen in a tendency to spend money, change plans, and enact new schemes at very short notice. These difficulties may not be apparent to the person with ADHD himself, but may cause great problems to family and co-workers.

Many adults with ADHD suffer because of poor memory. Many come to rely on aids such as writing everything down and placing reminders all over their homes and workplaces.

Another common area of difficulty is in self-appraisal. Adults with ADHD are often very inaccurate in their self-observation. They may have little idea of the impact that they are having on other people. This does not mean that they lack concern. They often have a tendency to worry needlessly about things. Many complain about a sense of impending doom or insecurity. Mood swings are also common.

The problems with self-esteem described in Chapter 7 may persist into adulthood. Many of the co-morbid emotional disorders also persist, and some degree of depression is therefore common in adults with residual ADHD.

In some adults with residual ADHD, risk-taking behavior is a problem. Such individuals search for high stimulation. In some cases this may be found in activities such as sport or public life. There is also a tendency toward addictive behavior, such as substance abuse, or activities such as gambling.

It can be seen that adults with ADHD are 'high risk' individuals. Many of their attributes may cause them to be extremely successful and to become 'high flyers'. However, they are also in danger of experiencing problems in personal relationships and with their financial affairs.

How is the diagnosis of residual ADHD made?

Many of the characteristics of residual ADHD are seen in normal adults. Everyone can be, to some extent, distractible, restless, and impulsive. The diagnosis of residual ADHD depends upon the duration and intensity of these problems, as well as the characteristic clustering of features.

The diagnosis may then be confirmed by psychometric and other testing similar to that carried out in children with suspected ADHD.

ADHD always starts in childhood. It is therefore a prerequisite for the diagnosis that the characteristics have been present throughout the person's life. In some cases, the diagnosis of ADHD will have already been made during childhood, but sometimes the diagnosis is first made in adulthood.

If it is clear that a child with ADHD will continue to have problems during adulthood, the pediatrician who looks after him will refer him to a psychiatrist once the child reaches adulthood (some pediatricians continue to treat individuals who were in their care into early adulthood). An adult who thinks he may have ADHD should request that his general practitioner refer him to a psychiatrist for an assessment.

Certain psychiatrists have a particular interest in residual ADHD and therefore have experience and expertise in this area. They may work in conjunction with psychologists who carry out standardized testing to evaluate the individual's particular strengths and weaknesses.

It is very important that the psychiatrist excludes other conditions that may mimic ADHD. Problems such as depression (sadness, low self-esteem, withdrawn behavior), mania (euphoria, overactivity, risk-taking), and obsessive-compulsive disorder, need to be excluded. Some of these are similar to ADHD, but the treatment is different.

Treatment of residual ADHD

Individuals with residual ADHD often have difficulties in a number of areas of their lives. Gaining insight into their problem makes a big difference to their ability to cope with these difficulties. Understanding that the problems arise from ADHD often makes it easier for the individual's partner and other members of the family to cope. The first step in treatment, therefore, is a proper explanation of the nature of residual ADHD and how it affects the person's functioning.

Some adults with ADHD require nothing more than this kind of explanation. However, many will need help in the form of medication and/or counseling.

Medication plays a vital role in helping a person with residual ADHD. The adult brain responds just as well as the child's brain to medications used for ADHD. Often the doses needed during adulthood are proportionately smaller than those needed for children. For example, an adult may need to take no more Ritalin (methylphenidate) or dexamphetamine per day than a primary school child, despite being considerably heavier.

An adult will need to administer the medication himself, and so issues relating to abuse of these medicines must be understood. With proper controls over the dispensing of medicines such as Ritalin and dexamphetamine, problems with dependence should not occur. The doses of these medicines used in ADHD are extremely small, and do not result in any change in mood that would encourage dependence.

All of the medicines used for children with ADHD can be used in adulthood. Anti-depressant medication may be very useful in adults with ADHD who also have depression. In such cases, higher doses of these medicines are used to obtain an anti-depressant effect.

Individual or group therapy can also be very helpful for adults with ADHD. In many cases, family therapy or marital guidance will also be helpful. Adults with ADHD commonly need help in finding ways of resolving inter-personal conflicts and in addressing marital, family, and occupational problems. Methods for anger control, treatment of addiction, improving self-esteem, and refining inter-personal skills are very useful.

Because of the organizational difficulties experienced by adults with residual ADHD, the teaching of time management and self-organizational skills is very helpful. Cognitive therapy, where the adult learns how to control thought patterns, is very successful in well-motivated adults with ADHD. Social problem-solving and stress reduction can be taught through counseling and role-playing. Group meetings can be helpful, and also provide mutual support and an opportunity to exchange ideas on managing common problems.

Treatment of secondary problems

Many adults with residual ADHD have problems with basic academic skills that date from their school days. These may be present even if the ADHD difficulties have resolved. There are many ways in which an adult with such difficulties can take steps to overcome them.

It is important to use the aids that are available. If attending lectures, a tape recorder can be used. If difficulties are experienced in taking notes, a friend may be prepared to use carbon paper or make a photocopy of his notes. A computer program may be used to check spelling. An electric typewriter or computer can be used to help produce work that is legible and well presented. For those who are better at typing than writing, there are portable computers and digital diaries. Calculators are portable and have made arithmetic calculations easy for everyone. Spelling dictionaries, both electronic and in book form, are helpful for adults who have spelling difficulties.

For those who have to take examinations, it is usually possible to arrange for allowances to be made for difficulties with reading or writing. It may be necessary to have a letter from a doctor or psychologist to obtain permission to use aids such as a typewriter, scribe, tape recorder, or spelling dictionary.

Those who continue to have difficulties with reading may benefit from 'talking books' (recordings of book readings), which are available from many libraries. Some libraries have books written for adults that are easy to read.

Adults who have difficulty with reading or writing should not be embarrassed to ask others to fill in forms for them. Many adults with good literacy skills experience difficulty with forms. Similarly, when taking messages, there is no reason to be embarrassed about asking to have things repeated or spelt out.

If an adult with ADHD is undertaking further training, he should inform his lecturers or teachers about his condition, in order that allowances can be made for his difficulties. Most universities have special provisions for the enrolment of people with disability and adults with ADHD often qualify for these.

Conclusion

All parents want their children to fulfil their academic potential, to be socially successful, and to be well adjusted emotionally. Tragically, many intelligent children fail in one or more of these areas. Although there are a number of reasons why this may happen, many do so because they have ADHD.

The best management of ADHD is based on early and accurate diagnosis, as outlined in this book. From this diagnostic process an individualized, multi-modal treatment plan can be developed for each child with the condition.

There is no doubt that more and more children with ADHD are receiving appropriate diagnosis and treatment. But the task of ensuring that all children with this condition benefit from a modern approach to their difficulties is far from complete. To ensure that this occurs, a widespread change in attitudes to children with behavioral, learning, and emotional difficulties is needed. We will need to move away from automatically blaming children and their families for children's learning and behavioral difficulties. We will need to understand that the brain is the organ of learning, of self-esteem, of behavior, and of emotion. We will need to be open to the possibility that an inefficiency in brain function may be the cause of many children's difficulties. We will need to treat ADHD with the same conviction that we presently treat conditions such as asthma and diabetes. With such changes, many more children will be able to look forward to a future of happiness and fulfilment.

Appendix — useful internet sites

Unfortunately the internet contains a great deal of misinformation about ADHD. The following sites are generally reliable:

http://www.chadd.org

CHADD (Children and Adults with ADHD), is a large US organization. Their website contains a great deal of reliable information about all aspects of ADHD. CHADD runs regular ADHD conferences in the US.

http://www.add.org

The US organization, ADDA (Attention Deficit Disorder Association), has an excellent website with reliable information. ADDA runs regular ADHD conferences in the US.

http://www.addwarehouse.com

An excellent site for those wanting to order books, videos, and tapes about ADHD.

http://www.additudemag.com

The 'Additude' magazine is an attractive and informative publication for those with ADHD and their families. This is the website of the magazine's publisher and it shares the magazine's positive tone.

http://www.adhd.com

This site provides a great deal of information and support. It has a 'Parents Place' as well as a section for adults with ADHD. It also contains an excellent discussion forum.

http://www.add.about.com

A subsection of the 'About.Inc' website, this section is devoted to providing information about ADHD.

http://www.addiss.co.uk

This is the website of ADDISS (The ADD Information and Support Service) in the UK. The site contains a great deal of information about conferences, support groups, and other resources in the UK.

http://www.adders.org

An informative and enterprising website set up by a UK couple who have a child with ADHD.

http://www.chaddcanada.org

This site has a great deal of information about Canadian services.

Index